Words to God's Music

Words to God's Music

A NEW BOOK OF PSALMS

Laurance Wieder

WILLIAM B. EERDMANS PUBLISHING COMPANY
GRAND RAPIDS, MICHIGAN / CAMBRIDGE, U.K.

Wm. B. Eerdmans Publishing Co.
255 Jefferson Ave. S.E., Grand Rapids, Michigan 49503 /
P.O. Box 163, Cambridge CB3 9PU U.K.

Printed in the United States of America

07 06 05 04 03   7 6 5 4 3 2 1

Library of Congress Cataloging-in-Publication Data

Bible. O.T. Psalms. English. Wieder. 2003
    Words to God's music: a new book of Psalms / Laurance Wieder.
        p.   cm.
    Includes bibliographical references.
    ISBN 0-8028-6089-3 (cloth: alk. paper)
        I. Wieder, Laurance, 1946-   II. Title.

    BS1424.W54   2003
    223'.205209 — dc21

                                                    2003044951

www.eerdmans.com

Contents

vi

❦

Contents

BOOK TWO: THE MOUNTAIN SOUND

Psalms 42–72

viii

∞

Contents

BOOK THREE: NOT YOU AND NOT THOSE THINGS

Psalms 73–89

BOOK FOUR: WHERE WE HAVE ALWAYS LIVED
Psalms 90–106

BOOK FIVE: RETURN. PROMISE.

Psalms 107–150

xiii

∞

Contents

Acknowledgments

Particular thanks to my friends Jody Bottum and David Shapiro, and to my wife and daughter, Andrea K. and Aiah Wieder, for their love and support.

Grateful acknowledgment is also made to the editors of the following publications, in which a number of these poems first appeared:

Books & Culture: "Follow?" (Psalm 46); "Who Else?" (Psalm 147)

Boulevard: "Deafened" (Psalm 74); "Shake" (Psalm 77)

Chronicles: "Old" (Psalm 71); "First" (Psalm 146); "Hope" (Psalm 72)

Commonweal: "Very" (Psalm 4); "Just Below" (Psalm 8)

First Things: "Doubletalk" (Psalm 12); "Gifted" (Psalm 21); "Express" (Psalm 31); "For Show" (Psalm 34); "Canopy" (Psalm 63); "As If" (Psalm 73); "Come" (Psalm 80); "Open" (Psalm 81); "Inheritance" (Psalm 82); "Willing" (Psalm 85); "Of State" (Psalm 86); "Recognition" (Psalm 139); "Distinction" (Psalm 143); "Mosaic" (Psalm 144); "Who Else?" (Psalm 147)

Pequod: "Dumb" (Psalm 49)

Scripsi: "The Beast" (Psalm 18); "Mask" (Psalm 89); "An Alphabet" (Psalm 119); Pilgrim Psalms (Psalms 120-134)

The following poems appeared in *The Poets' Book of Psalms*

(published by HarperCollins in 1995): Psalm 9, Psalm 21, Psalm 33, Psalm 39, Psalm 53, Psalm 107, Psalm 109, Psalm 118, Psalm 120, and Psalm 149.

xvi

∞

Acknowledgments

A Brief Explanation

The Bible's Book of Psalms ranges across history, and speaks to both the eternal and the immediate, living moment. Although the Talmudic sages identify its 150 songs with ten authors, the book as a whole is attributed to the shepherd and singer King David, who was as close as anyone ever came to being perfect in the eye of God. His songs of the heart are canonical for all the major faiths and sects — Jewish, Christian, and Islamic.

Poets have been translating the Psalms for as long as poems have been written in English. Their number includes mighty if not always orthodox believers like John Milton and George Herbert, men of the world like Ben Jonson, and luminous doubters like Samuel Taylor Coleridge and Lord Byron.

Counting the Elizabethan duet of Mary Herbert and her courtier brother Philip Sidney as one, and the enthusiastic Christopher Smart, who was committed to Bedlam after repeatedly falling to his knees in the streets of London and inviting passersby to pray with him, I am (to the best of my knowledge) only the third poet to produce a complete English version of the Songs of David.

Poets' versions differ from psalms found in translations of the Bible, and from the metrical psalms found in hymnals. Bible versions owe their first allegiance to the letter of the text, and its authority. They think about doctrine, and edition, and history even as they are being born, often in committee. Metrical psalms were written to fit received melodies for singing. They frequently have a sectarian cast, such as Isaac Watts's New Testament Psalms — which were answered from the Old Testament side by his friend Cotton Mather's *Psalterium Americanum*.

Poetry feeds on history, and strife, and music, on language and on that flow of minute particulars which adds up to life lived. A poem's authority derives not from tradition or legalism, but from its directness, vitality, and beauty. Sometimes to excess. The King James Version of Psalm 148:3 reads, ". . . praise him, all ye stars of light." Thomas Stanley, in his version of the same, talks to the stars directly:

xviii

A
Brief
Explanation

Roses of gold on azure sown,
You sparkling jewels of the night,
Who silently encamp unknown,
Your squadrons in their tents of light;
Whom the militia of the skies
In several factions doth bestow,
To kindle war, which spreading, flies
Throughout our lesser world below —
Praise him by whom you shall at last be thrown
To earth, and forced to lay your bright arms down.

Poems also have formal qualities. Form may be the first thing that catches the reader's eye, as in Mary Sidney Herbert's version of Psalm 117:

P raise him that aye
R emains the same:
A ll tongues display
I ehovah's fame.
S ing all that share

T   his earthly ball:
H   is mercies are
E   xposed to all:
L   ike as the word
O   nce he doth give,
R   olled in record,
D   oth time outlive.

Or a work may be so well wrought that its technique is transparent. The outward observation of traditional verse forms does not guarantee a poem's virtue, nor does an apparent freedom automatically impeach it.

Older poetry sometimes demands a lot of work to get past those conventions that encrust the living part. Spelling has always been a slippery field, even after the eighteenth century, when the letter *I* was no longer interchangeable with the letter *J*. Vocabulary and grammar shift; words and what they stand for drop out of fashion, or out of sight. Though with a little trouble, it's possible to make out both the real distress and the first verse of Psalm 102 ("Hear my prayer, O Lord, and let my cry come unto thee") in the opening lines of Thomas Wyatt's poetry paraphrase:

> Lord hear my prayer, and let my cry pass
> Unto the Lord without impediment.
> Do not from me turn thy merciful face,
> Unto myself leaving my government.

By the same token, contemporary speech can quickly lose its resonance and sharp looks. Through the applications of art, including tact and taste, poetry ages well. Or as Christopher Smart puts it in his version of Psalm 127,

∽

A
Brief
Explanation

If the work be not direct,
> And the Lord the fabric build,
All the plans that men project
> Are but labor idly spilled.

In the early 1990s, I collaborated on *Chapters into Verse,* an anthology of poetry inspired by the Bible. The experience changed me. Reading unfamiliar works by familiar poets (whose Bible poems were often printed at the back of their collected works, apart from their "real" poetry), as well as otherwise neglected minor poets of scriptural rather than literary note, taught me to expect more of poetry than an aesthetic jolt. It also reminded me that didactic verse does not necessarily delight or instruct. Poetry is more musical and also knows more than prose. When it fuses music and meaning, tenderness and authority, poetry can be the written image of a shepherd and a king.

Following *Chapters into Verse,* I decided to assemble as a literary anthology the complete Book of Psalms using poets' versions. Although I had many to choose among for the more "popular" psalms — at least twelve for Psalm 23; six for Psalm 121; and sixteen for Psalm 137 — for long stretches the only possible entries were by one of the Sidneys or by Christopher Smart. To inject a little twentieth-century variety into what threatened to become an antiquarian enterprise, I translated my first psalm (Psalm 53, "The Fool Says to Himself"). Having done one, I tried doing more. Doing more, I decided to do all.

Some of these poems live fairly close to their biblical originals; others are best described as accounts in English of events in another language; others stand as commentaries or variations upon the text. To prepare, I read all the English versions, poetic and otherwise; I read Martin Luther's German and P. Hately

Waddell's Scots. I read the *Midrash on Psalms*. I did what I could with Jerome's Latin, and of course *Tehillim*. Then I wrote, usually with Mitchell Dahood's Anchor Bible *Psalms* beside the keyboard, open to the notes.

Whenever I could manage it, I made acrostics and anagrams and alphabets corresponding to those in the Hebrew. I followed the Sidneys in reducing the English alphabet to the twenty-two letters of the Hebrew (as in Psalm 119). I wrote the 18th Psalm as a miniature epic. Rather than try to improve what can't be improved, I composed a midrash on the 23rd Psalm. I divided these 150 psalms into five books, to reflect the traditional fivefold division of the Hebrew.

My father asked me recently, "What's the difference between a poem and a psalm? A psalm's a poem, isn't it?"

I answered that outwardly a psalm and a lyric poem are the same. They differ in how they speak, and to whom.

A lyric poem always happens in the first-person voice of the poet, even when the "I say" is only implicit, even if the "I" is an assumed voice and not the actual poet's.

The Bible's psalms, on the other hand, are songs of David, the singer and second King of Israel, even when composed by one of the psalmists or musicians associated with his court, because (as it says in the *Midrash*) "his is the sweetest voice of all."

Lyric poems address another person, or place, or thing. They are the occasion of speech to the beloved, to the grammatical object, to the reader. They excite admiration. When the poet's voice is heard directly, unmediated, like a voice on the other end of the phone that invites a response, then a poem lives and is understood.

The Psalms address God and the eternal. Outside of history, and beside the passage of time, the psalm waits for the reader, who speaks through the psalm, which becomes the language of the reader's heart. The psalmist asks for, complains of, praises, or repents; neither he nor those who speak with and through him expect an answer. The response is inward.

Two examples should make this plainer.

In "Ozymandias" Shelley reports, "I met a traveler from an antique land/Who said: 'Two vast and trunkless legs of stone/Stand in the desert. . . .'" Here the "I" is the poet, listening to another's first-person tale. The reader sits down with the poet and listens along. For the space of a sonnet, writer and reader inhabit the same historical moment, and participate in the same awe: "Look on my works, ye Mighty, and despair!" The poem is an object, with a subject.

A psalm is understood differently. The psalmist's "I" escapes from history, from doctrine, and speaks for anyone and everyone who reads his lines. When I read "The Lord is my shepherd, I shall not want," I understand that means my shepherd, as well as David's; that the utterance holds true right now as well as in the time of Samuel; my heart says so today, and also tomorrow. "Surely goodness and mercy shall follow me all the days of my life. . . ." To say it is to believe it. The words of the psalm become my words, too.

These psalms are not the last or only word on the Psalms, in any language. I wrote them out of the conviction that there really was poetry, as I understand the word, in the Songs of David — something more delightful than their great authority, which shines through every version.

These poems can be read along with a Bible; they can be read on their own. They are my answer to the received dissonance between sincerity and poetry, between the letter and the spirit of the law.

Book One   ONE WILL BLOSSOM

∽   Psalms 1–41

1 *The Happy One*

The happy one steers clear of lawyers,
    Steps aside for party-goers,
Sits apart from mouthy mockers,
    Loves to learn the Lord's lore:
He turns the Lord's laws over night and day,
    A gardener tilling holy ground.
And the happy one will blossom
    Like the fruit trees in a watered field
Bearing plum peach walnut pear and apple
    Cupped by green leaves the long season,
Harvest bushels crated by the orchard.

Not the faithless. They are dead leaves,
    Clippings flattered by the wind,
Who cannot judge themselves
    Much less the happy, and must stand
Apart. Lord knows how
    The good make their way,
But the bad go and come in darkness.

3

∞

One
Will
Blossom

2 Kiss It

Why strangers rage
For power, harvest forests massing
   Fleets like clouds
   Hulls over water,
Uncoil lines to hoist their bellied
   Sails, singing:
   "Heave, the wind
   Will make us kings,"

I can't say, but the oceans roar
   Blue laughter
   At them, of the trade
Winds, of the seething maker
   Who said before
And after pouring oil on the son,
   The daughter:

   "Child, ask.
It will be given: anything:
   A pot to keep
   The heavens
   In, or smash
To earth, hopes dashed."

So I say: Time. Tie up those trains
   That trail dust:
   Kiss the child
Come to life, or he will grow up
   Angry. Make it
   Better. Anyway,
   Flash and perish.

3   *Yet*

Lord, there are more
Of them than of me.
They say,
      No help for him.

I say,
    When I call out
The hills rebound more
Than an echo. You hear me.   5

∞

I lay down, and sleeping   *One*
Dreamed a crowd roared   *Will*
Around me.
      Their teeth crack.   *Blossom*

4   *Very*

Look at this!
A circle dance
Around a bonfire
That won't stop,
They swear,
Until rain falls.
If dance can make rain fall,
Tears might make rain.
If they could see
What fools they are,
Their wheatfields might
Be watered, and wine flow.
    But no.
        I sleep.
You bring the clouds.

5 Give a Moment

Here's what I think:
Each morning I stretch between good
    Ways and evil thoughts,
Pleasure and fools who choose pain
    For their portion.
Like God, I hate liars who murmur
    Mere pleasantries, forge
Shackles of paper: "Do what I tell you or else
    Taste destruction."
No one can destroy me with threats. Although
    Sleeping a bad man
Imagines his strength has grown boundless, and I
    The meat shoveled
Into his mouth, witless tool of his private design,
    I'm not touched.
But that fool gets taken in by himself
    And thrown out.

7

∞

One
Will
Blossom

6 Pent

Don't hit, don't hurt me
More, I'm shaken lower
Than my bones could know,
Cracked terror of God's
Anger at my errors. So

What if I cried into my pillow
From right now until I died?
Would I find happiness?
Do the dead decry their emptiness
Or sing for you, for good?

Scavengers mistook my tears
For weakness: when one finger
Stirs, the dainty vultures flap
Their weighty feathers. Faced
With life, they scatter.

One thing to trust the person
Seated at my left, or right:
That's left to chance and lions'
Natures — they may not have
    Right instincts, save
To stalk, to spring, to savage.

Meek enough, but still not meat,
I have to trust what I know
Of another, have to show
My sunny side, my peach
To one I choose, or hope to touch,
Whose heart I hope to reach.

But friends can foil, bare the tooth,
Claw, snarl, scratch, bite when I turn
My eye away, or when I sleep. Lord,
Take the lion hunter and the lion
In the pit one dug for the other.
    Let me sing on trust.

8   Just Below

Although we cannot say your name
Aloud, both earth and sky
Hang moving pictures of your present,
Giving children speech and strength
To quiet even angry strangers.
When I look at the sky, the night sky
Moonlit, starred with patterns
That go past me, I wonder

What we are, that you take notice?
Or our children, who can sing
Songs we've forgotten? We stand

Just below angels, who see glory,
Honor as we do those fields, trees,
Mountains, chasms, rivers, oceans
You have given us sway over:
Grazing herds and feral stalkers,
Creatures of the house and barnyard,
Songbirds, shorebirds, fish, whatever
Swims or sails through the deep.
Yet all these goods spread out
Before us, for generations,
Do not begin to sound one syllable
Of what the whole earth knows
Best left unsaid.

9 Personal

If I could tell it all,
I would say thank you
For the toppled statues,
For the dusk of gods sung
Only in dead languages,
For wild grapevines tangled
In the timbers of a century
That frame our little picture
Of eternity. And I remember
There was justice, maybe, since
I hope the dead might be
Remembered, though their names,
Outnumbered by the stones
Once used to mark the exit spot,
Are worn down, in an alphabet
That can't be read aloud.

Not always and not ever, maybe
Masters will stick in the mud
Of what they most admired,
Boasting how their acts
Engraved in stone erased
Accounts of people sacrificed
To feed the maw, the pointless
Grim machinery of nations:
If there is something other
Than our selves, they will not win
Forever, will some time remember
They are human, and may even
Know themselves, and feel afraid.

10 Foul

Aloof, in hiding, Lord,
When schemers step out
From dark corners and, piling
What they want upon their plate,
Dig in? They get their way,
And fear no thing, the violent
Ones who gobble down
A course of blood and curses.

No longer haunting alleys,
Poised by open doorways,
He swaggers at the corner
In broad daylight, marking
Out his prey from passers-by,
Saying, "God looks far
Away, God has forgotten."

Enough. Raise your hand
Against them, Lord,
Answer those cacklers
Who count upon you
Not paying back.
Break off their legs, wings, hopes.
Let them have ours.

11 Cheers

I trust. You can't say
To my soul, fly away
From the park
Bench into treetops,
Aiming darts at my heart.
I can't help what
The others do, but
I stand up straight
In full view. Those haters
Must wait for their cup
To be passed, and drink up.

13

❦

One
Will
Blossom

12   *Doubletalk*

Turn where?
    Hear
Shark hearts, the fast
Talking, two-faced,
The beasts boast:
    Truth
    Trips and
    Falls on
    My lips:
    If I say
    It is so
    It is so.

If God's word be hot
Coal (my good thoughts
The embers),
    Lord,
Stoke up a bonfire.
Those lip-lickers lurk
In the shadows
    And eye me.

13 Unlucky

Forget me? Forever? How long
Without smiling? How long
Must I talk to myself, with my heart
Heavy freight? Must I wait
For the haters to hoot at my funeral?
For my eyes to be draped
With black velvet sleep death?
Hear me, O Lord, not for me
But for your sake,
So the bad cannot boast
Over me and my troubles. I trust
You have heard me, will
Care for me, spare me
So I can sing songs of how long
You remembered.

15

∞

One
Will
Blossom

14   Plantation

"There is no God."
The fool speaks from his heart
   And bends his back
And sees black loam where God
   Looks down
And sees no good at all,
   Just dirt
Disguised as great ones, plotters
   Selling others'
Fruit. But worms will turn.
   Some day
The poor will wipe that proud
   Fool's smile
Off his face, and pin him fast.
   An angel
Wrestled Jacob to a draw.

15 Barely

The minimum?
    Say what you mean.
    Do what you say.
Point no finger at another.
    Welcome strangers,
    Not strange dealers.
Never waver.
    Feed the hungry.
    Charge no interest: or
The minimum.

∞

One
Will
Blossom

16   Balance

Because I said: One God, no true religion,
    And do not worship
Money, altars, rites, and idols people
    Make to dazzle
Certain but not self believers, nor dice
    Thrown, nor letters
Cloaking brutal grasping, I enjoyed
    A fortune, telling
Praises by the names of things
    And of the nameless
Steady in the dark: at the pit's edge
    I won't teeter, ever.

17   *Yes*

My heart had a visitor come in the night:
No moonbeam in gauze robe, nor sweet-scented raptor:
But straight-talking, heartfelt, so turn a good ear:

I've watched strong men work shovel and pickax,
Saw, hammer, and nails. Cursed, they build steel
Towers for others. But I call to you, and you hear.

You hear me, surrounded by goat-headed hoodlums,
Loudmouths and lions too young to be gentle.
I think my soft song must be better than roaring.

You heard from the shelter of apple tree shadows
And gave me a home life, the hope of small children,
Unbroken sleep with no thought of the others, and

Mornings I wake looking like, looking at you.

19

∞

One
Will
Blossom

18   The Beast

The strength that comes lifting weights
From my heart
Comes from the other world
Beyond my self:
Seeing the concrete city of knowing,
Not of dreaming.

Death and sadness, sex and violence
Lured me, scared me
And I called aloud to the park sky,
To the starless night,
To corner crossers, legal vendors,
Paper readers:

None heard the music God
Plays, that elastic
Being: yet the mighty other turned
All ear: the empty
Subway platform shook, oaks willowed,
Highways buckled.

Before me roared leviathan of old,
His mouth a stadium
Whose bleacher gates spat crowds
Of smoke and fire
Streamed between tiered clouds,
Whose feet

Trod the black sky, which came apart

Like sea grass
Parts for horsemen at the gallop.
His wings were wind.
His tail twitched the way a stalking cat's
Flicks side to side,

A peril to its prey. Or when neap tide
Rolls back, and people
Stroll on what had been the sea bed,
We walk on secrets,
Run for cover when with snorts and
Flashes clouds bear down.

Because I just believed that I could
Change my heart,
Not how the other people were,
Not when I came
Or go from here, I didn't snarl
Hope and fear

And saw a way around the trap
Of slave life, bound
To needless need and anger, greed,
The appetites
That grow the more they feed,
A sad ambition.

I see that most of what I see's
Inside me:
So the merciful see mercy;
The honest one

∞

Finds honesty around him.
The bad ones

Live in their own schemes,
Duped by desires
Cold rain can't douse, and shiver, soaked
While others shelter
Under the high tree and wonder
At the storm.

There is a light. By its beams
I pass through crowds
Across the barricades, past rock,
Up gravel paths
With switchbacks to an overlook,
Commanding

The high ground, which gently
Slopes away,
Where I can see whole generations
Turn to dust
Who have tormented me,
And hear their cries

But need not heed them. Rumors
Of the Lord
Bestow more power than poetry
Sung by an unbeliever,
Than hours billed by lawyers
To defend the wrong,

And I have found such temper
In those judgments
I have left to time, as praise gives
To the prayer,
Ruler over first myself,
Then blessings:

Children, animals, a home
To salve the sore
Points, peeves that threatened
Both the singer
And his lilting, which might last
A little more.

∞

One
Will
Blossom

19   Canter

　　　　Big, shy, a schoolboy
Canters laps around the ballfield,
A dapple colt escaped both dam and stable
Grazing the green theater of his being.
To see it clearly's sweet as sunlight
On an autumn shoulder, shining on the face
Of harder laws than stadiums in stone.
I learned a lot just sitting in the bleachers:
To understand, and not mistake, my own
Words for the breath that makes me pause.
God, give me enough light and will
　　　　To say just what I see,
　　　　　　See what I do,
　　　　　　Do what I say,
　　　　　　Say what you will.

24

∞

Book

One

20 *Yay*

Outside the walls, a roaring crowd might be
The sound of natural catastrophe,
And borne as any freak of chance
Dealt evenly, but when a mob chants
Slogans, hates in unison, that one mind
Thinks a hell for all who do not share
The thought. Banners need wind
To float. In calm, they fold and die.

I sat up straight. I spoke up quietly
Of the unspoken name that baffles wind
On the past's window, and hope's pillow.

25

∞

One
Will
Blossom

21 Gifted

The haves shall have and have more
Than they ask, will live a long time,
Winter in palm sunshine,
Watch herons fish the squall line
And be neither fish, nor fowl, but eye,
A cup to taste immensity.

The others drink December polar murk.
They listen for the furnace switch, the pilot
Light, hot water pump: the damned could stick
No closer to their fires. Outside, the wind
Drives a person back into himself, where
All he knows is what he has imagined.

22 *Wanting*

Alone. No help. But why so far?
To damp my roaring? Day or night,
Still out of earshot, tired of hearing
My complaint? But you're not crushed.
My father's father's father trusted
From his lamplit study, and was not
Unready. So I am less observant,
Less in learning, than the old ones. Smirkers
Bother now to point the finger. Teeth bared,
Lip curled, they shake their heads and mutter:
That one trusted in disorder, in the great
Provider: let his providence deliver him.

But you delivered me into the world,
Made hope the milk I drank, cradled me
Between your elbow crook and wrist,
Held up my head until I found my strength.
Support me now, when troubles
Ring me, paw like highland bulls, snort
Steam and heave fat divots with their hooves.
You must be near, must pick me up
And give me strength to save my life from bitterness.

If I have blown the horn of what I have imagined
To be true, it came from you. And shuddered.
Fear is praise to one who shows his face,
Who hears his name called in an empty place,
A name not known. Who but the meek
Could eat and not want more? The fat sit down

27

∞

*One
Will
Blossom*

At groaning tables and remember to recall their souls.
While every time a world ends, seeds
Drop in the dust, then sprout, and someone
Else is born to care for what's beyond
Bad dreams. I live. The unborn queue.

23   *Solo*

I want no shepherd when I lie
Down, don't need to be led to water, shade
   Or rest. One who restores
Souls can't be lost forever. Death and truth
   Are names for what we living do not
Know, but fear as much as what may not
   Be said. No trouble now to sit
Down with my enemy. He too must chew.
     We dip our bread in oil.
    Wine splashes over the cup's lip.
Good within surrounds me, certain life
    Is all I ever know.

29

∞

One
Will
Blossom

24 Numerous

Jacob lay down in the waste
And slept, dreamed, woke, and shook, and saw
The ground he stood on had a name.

Currents on the open ocean, wells
Below blank sand, magnetic concentrations
Cloaked by ice, deep-space ionic winds:

∞

No where is empty, full with names
For namelessness. Get up. The door
Can never shut. Any door lets angels
    Go and come.

25 Abracadabra

Raise my sights above the heads
Of babblers, grabbers, gloaters,
So I don't blush at the mirror;
Let me hear and say some portion
    Of the pointed version.
To get it right, I stumbled over laces, walked,
Then ran. Now I want to go on farther
And so walk again. I remember how.
When fears bare tree limb shadows
Stab across the picket fence, I trust
    They'll pass. I trust
The sun will rise tomorrow. Promises,
For children ask their parents' parents
    "What will we inherit?"
Only to turn back to playing Fish or War,
With no time for the answer:
    "All that's left."
Earth's cramped by pushy phantoms:
For them the past and what is coming pass
As certainty. Frets maybe, for a picker
Out of melodies that start and end "Poor me,"
But no tune for the child of what is real.

Judge me, trust me,
Test me, weigh me,
Love me, for my heart's
    Desire:
Hated idols, merit stealers,
Brushed off greedy dumbbells, dealers,
Washed my hands of hired
    Liars.
Take me with the heartfelt thinkers,
Talkers for the truth, far seers,
Etchers of the royal real mover's
    Picture.

God is difficult
To see, and near.
What's left to fear?
When cannibals
Pound on my door,
    I'm steady.
All I ask: to live
    In God's house,
Soul in body,
High ground tent pitched,
    Singing:
Hear me, answer.
    I watch water,
    Calm and stirred up
    As a picture
    Of your face.
I saw and can't forget it:
    Parents left me;
    What I knew
    For true stayed
      With me,
    So I pass
Between my enemies
    Like songs through trees,
Past liars sworn against me,
By eaters up of merit.
    I hold my peace.
    I learned to wait.

33

∞

One
Will
Blossom

28 Rock

I call out to the rock:
It calls back as a rock
Dropped into a chasm
Reports from the deep.

Then I picked up a stone
For the loudmouth, the bully,
The whey-faced cheater
And splitter of hairs.

Your stone-slinging psalm singer,
Sweeter than centuries,
You hear me, and feed us,
And love us forever.

The wind draws longhand script on open water:
One light breath scoots sparrow flocks of diamonds:
Gales halloo, stand great waves' hair on end, flip white
    forelocks
Back that first cracked cedar timbers hewn in Lebanon,
Pick up boulders skipped across the water, flat stones
Thrown by seashore boys, who then return
To watch their campfire fork, shake embers at the meteors
Of August or December sky, sing folk songs   *35*
About spring tides, forest days, how armies they imagine   ∞
Rode through rain, arked animals, sat out the flood, could talk
Of heat and light come from within, and mean it: summed   *One*
Less than a whisper of the Lord who thunders underneath   *Will*
    The backwash, in calm air.   *Blossom*

30 Reverse

Sick of not knowing what attacked me,
I looked outside. The floating world
Played words and pictures of my fear:
That clutch of names taught in a dream
Can be set down. And promises release.
I misconstrued both strength and weakness.
What good does anger at the dead do?
Sharp, polished, careful phrases cut
The mouth no lips would kiss, and
Playing sage or twenty questions is straight
Poker dealt to the abyss. Preoccupied, I missed
The top step, flapped my arms hard,
Shouted, "God!" and caught myself. Recovered
Balance, one of many dances clumsies do
        To chance made music.

31 Express

I'm here because I hated
Heedless worshippers of words but trust
A truth. I've known the eagle's and the worm's
Eye view, and am quite happy with one room
That's not a cell, have watched my muscles
Slack, my bones grown brittle, heard my stomach
Quease around an empty table. One forgotten
Cup crushed by the roadside, I hear them talk
As though I am not.
                    Your call, Lord. I am ashamed
For you, who might stop up their mouths with dirt
Who dare to puff and dandle lies about me.
Mercy traces hate like lightning through forked limbs
Scorching leaf and root: they thought God was a tree,
Safe shelter from the winter thunderstorms.
I spoke too quickly when I cried forgotten.
I hear my thoughts above the clamored claims
Upon your ear, and you reply: I trust that life
Lets life go on. When time's up,
Life lets go.

32 Understand

Guilt hidden
Maddens.
Madness:
The affront
To sense.
Innocence:
The lash, or
Rumor
Spurring
Candor.
Unbending
Oaks crack,
Willows
Beside rivers
Hardly ever.

33   History

There is no new thing in God's sight.
(The day, the moon, are new to us.)
Play a new song to the Lord,
Glass full enough to pass along
       Without a spill.
       Such ink made sky black,
    Kissed stars through pinholes, caught
Their night tears in a jar, each drop an ocean.

"Let be there was" — the deep mind stamped
A pattern on the nothing of before
       What was to be stood forth:
When time, one chord, struck there
       To now. Whatever
       One possesses
    Is a gift from elsewhere.
Inspiration comes unbidden.
       One guessed
At what's inside our nature.
Truth stays hidden, feeds upon
       The question.
       Some try to steal
A march on death, drown fear in senses.
Some chosen can believe the soul is real.

34 For Show

Today I have to dance, hoo-ha, roast lamb,
How summer's put to bed, no supper
After beast boys boasting pass the dipper.
No, I'll never say it. Never.
Kings could call me clever,
Show their wives wares favors

Toasty, pour the empty bottle
40   Over here please. I sing psalms just

To the thread that holds it all together,
Harp in hand, my knees and head
Elected by the dust to rule the doodle-do.

Lord, if I am crazy let me be so in name
Only. Haters, eaten from the inside out,
Ride slowly with their lawyers toward the exit
Door, and think it not there, but there is no out.

Lord, be my attorney   blow back my attackers
The winds make your argument   time is your courtroom
Defend me from pit men   their dank roadside ditches
Hide traps laid for passers-by   even the innocent
Grease their tracks, spin them   through slithery oil slicks
Into the sumps they've dug   hold their heads under
Then hear my bones shout   "Public Defender
No tongue for hire, he   parries the spoilers"
Bring on your witnesses   perjurers, peepers, claiming
They know me, those   strange to themselves

Though I feel sadly at others'   bad tidings, the owls
Hoot, jeer, mock when   told of my trouble
Enter my plea, now   my head's in a lion's mouth
Stripped, in a stadium   jurymen pointing, shout
"There he is, look at him"   God, stick their words
Down their throats   make them swallow hard
Wolves and accusers   convinced of my innocence
Then bring in the verdict   their shame and confusion
Sunlight on courthouse steps   your law book my love song
Of praiseworthy practice   that's worthy to try

41

❧

One
Will
Blossom

36 Scale

Prophets whisper and a boom
Rolls from the mountains,
While the false can bellow
Like a bronze bull offered
Nothing by his worshippers
And not be heard.

Highness of the mountains
(And the clouds above them,
Moon and stars, and sun),
Hide what gapes beyond
From us; keep the climber
Looking to the cliff, not down

At those who had no footing.

Fighting ignorance is pulling
   Crabgrass from a lawn:
      A waste.
    Prune apple suckers,
     Dig with earthworms.
   Take the morning sun,
     And shade at lunch.

   The open hand gets filled,
    A grasping one goes empty,
Angry, swearing to what can't
   Be known. Look inside
   Proud houses: no one home.
The meek inherit, and delight
   While bad men grind their teeth
   Is just a joke God laughs at.
Better honest poor than greedy
Rich, though poor is always harder.
   Small need small want. The big,
   The grabbers, will be eaten
   As they eat, like burping
Mudbaths swallow up fat bathers.
   Greed borrows and defaults.
    The good give freely.

   I was young before
    And now am old:
    Who does not know
   The difference between men

43

∞

One
Will
Blossom

And women, right and wrong
    Will never know.
Although the bad seed towers
Like a slippery elm,
    Blight strips its leaves,
    The tree's cut down
And ground to mulch the base
Of other ornamentals
    Shading walks.

Brought up short:
It hurts to think I am alive,
  Bones stuck with arrows,
  Understanding botched
With guilt. My bedsores weep, skin slick,
Sheets billow from gut-wrenching wind.
Friends carry flowers, keep a distance,
  Napkins to their faces.
Those who hate me call my sickness
  Judgment. Is it?
  I heard nothing,
Would not see God spoke no longer.
I want to live, remembering my faults,
  Am ready not to be.
  If you are near, how
Many return good, or try to
  Follow something other
Than self-measure? Do the hateful
  Make their smiling matches
  Over tables, split
Sides with laughter and the check?
  Your joke. My body.
  Now, or never.

45

∞

One

Will

Blossom

39 Bridled

I said, I will watch my mouth
And made no comment even
On the good, and I was sad.
My heart raced, something hot
Inside me made me cry out loud:

God, let me know when I've begun
A thing, and when it will be done;
Let me know how my days will run
From hot and fat to dim, to fail
And fall without a flutter by your hand.

What's there to wait for? Money? Power?
What's there to hope for? Old age? Honor?
The mock of dimwits? Spoiled children?
Your finger pressed across my mouth.
My lovely self was flannel, time a moth.

Hear me. Don't be put off by tears.
I'm stranger and a nomad like my father.
Give me strength enough to rise, to speak,
To spill a glass of water on the tabletop before
I thirst, and sip, and am no more.

For years I wanted more
Than sky to hear me mutter
More than meditations on the dark
    Behind a wall. The cracks
On lake ice, wrinkled bells, had ways
    To praise. Better stories
No one asks for, than to execute
Commissioned essays about oil
    Paintings, strokes
Compelling taste adoring. Money
Offered is no different than blood
And mutton of burnt sacrifice,
Substantial but unmusical,
    A seashell out of ocean.

Do cities, hungry for confusion,
Wait upon the violent moment
    Written in a book?
They listen by the numbers, charts
And statues of the dire tales
Self-made giants call the real
World, a portrait of their nature
Worshipped. A volcano spews
Steam, ash, and coats its sides
With runny lava. Giants are not
    Gods. Why crave approval?
    Does a dogfish basking
In the shallows think, and wait
        To hear from me?

47

∞

One

Will

Blossom

41 Recovery

It's hard to talk about the poor and not mean
"Poor me." Some think the cure is the disease.
Perhaps, if knowledge comforted, and fortune
        Made no enemies.
Ninnies, calling sickness judgment,
Send for drugs to end my suffering,
And squabble over what I'll leave behind me.
Even friends I trusted eye their share of me
        That is to come.
I am not dumb. God, pity dictates
That you set my foot down on top
Of their heads, heavily, to stop
Their wagging tongues now, and indefinitely.

Book Two   THE MOUNTAIN SOUND

      ఌ   Psalms 42–72

A panting hart run to the desert
Brays for water, no stream near,
   And beagles, yipping, lap
   His customary spring.
My soul licks salt tears as the pack
     Gives tongue, baying,
     "Where is God?"
This vacant lot in earshot
Of cartwheels, tumblers, loose change at their festival.

    Why lose heart?
    Hear bottom now?
  I still can call out,
     Still praise him.
    Remember how dank rumbles
    Guttered through the deep;
     The mountain sound,
    Combers broke over me?
Come daylight see the dark night of my soul:

    O my rock,
   Can a rock be forgetting?
Is this night without starlight
   Death in my bones?
    "Where is God?"
  O, my soul's heavy rock
In a free fall, the wind of its drop
    Sounds like sighing.
Wait. Only wait. In the rush. God will come.

51

∞

The
Mountain
Sound

43 Tacit

Between myself and the cheat what's to choose?
   If I shrugged off strength and made gloom
My whole practice, cursed weakness in anger,
   Then I'd know no God but advantage.
O my soul, so unquiet. The wind drops. The hum.

44   Related

We've heard the story many times
Before, how our fathers
Came to be who they are, started early,
Made their money,
Married, built the houses we grew up in:
How they had to struggle
Against bigots, brokers, bankers, greedy nations;
They fought wars and won:
Signs they were God's boast, the chosen.
Our luck's turned bad.
Those lions have raised sheep, with none
To follow, shorn
And slaughtered, beaten as a sport
By clowns who spit
Out Israel, a catcall, in our faces.

Yet we remember in our hearts
And words, we walk
The path you've plotted, through snakepits,
Mobs and death camps,
Past skyless streets, down alleyways,
Brick air shafts. Here laws
Serve things, give reasons why they kill us.
God, you sleep?
Are people cast-off clothes, a habit
To be broken
With effort underneath the wheels
Of random trucks
And left as treadmarks in the dust?
Or help us, only
For the sake of your own name.

45 Daughter

If the matter's good, then manner hardly matters.
What's written in the heart a hand can copy quickly.
I love to look at you because no word escapes your lips
That was not written in your heart, and on your face.
So float majestically through life where others crawl:
Lies puff them up too large; truth keeps you small.
Because you love to do what's right, you deserve
The rare things: aloe soaps and lavender
Perfume, cedar closets full of skirts and dresses,
Silk shirts, buttons pearl and ivory, dainty
Speeches such as birds made Solomon.
        Listen, child, you will leave home
Gladly, without tears, to walk with whom you please,
And everyone will want to meet your happiness.
Rich men's daughters and free spirits, true companions
Fill your grown-up house, and children, many more
Than met your father, who remembers that he loves
        You, always, to himself, out loud.

46   *Follow?*

The earth is hollow, and has jaws.
Mountains topple whole into the ocean
      Heart, which boils, bubbles.
    Where I stand, a river turns
The heart into Jerusalem, a stream
      Of thought into God's house.
    Though day break, strange crowds enter roaring,
      Batter at the doorposts,
    The temple will not fall. Fear
Froze us in our tracks, but melted at a whisper:
      God is with us.
    Earth is full of life. Two broken
      Armies in the field
    Smoked destruction, engines dead,
      Cars turtled, spinning wheels.
    Silence comes before and after,
    In the empty space around us,
      And is with us.

55

∞

*The
Mountain
Sound*

47   *Formula*

One hand clap
Split the earth
When Korah's
Children jumped
Back from the crack.

Two lips press on
New Year's ram's horn.
Praise slips through clear air
That closes.

The holy city's built on Zion mountain.
Towers, walls encircle the high house.
      There, God speaks to us
So plainly armies filing through the waste can hear,
So ships from Tarshish riding anchor shudder,
Borne upon the rocks by an east gale.
We watched them break up from our city windows.

     Take a turn about the mountain,
Its towers built upon our fathers' ruins.
     Moses brought the law. His two hands
Held out life and good, and death and evil:
     Then taught what follows.

57

∞

The
Mountain
Sound

49   *Dumb*

The plainest words, gotten by my understanding,
Seem parables plucked on the muffled guitar string:

The ignorant don't follow why I'm not afraid
Of the purse proud, who boasts he's made
Billions but can't save himself or anyone
From age, disease, and death. Though he see
Jerks and movers, helpless knowers
Taken in mid-sentence, their heaps left to others,
He thinks to himself that the ball cannot
Level his house, strip the land he has named
For himself: many acres, tall towers.
                He will last
Like the dog lifts his leg on the cornerstone,
Leaves his mark, then is gone with no trace.
    But a man's not a dog.
    Children read what the dead said.

The good are flowers, trees grown
In rows over ranks of the dead,
Fruit blossoms fed by the grave.
A rich man's the bursting of seed pods,
Ripened to scatter on the next puff of wind.
Though, living, men praised him,
They also admire the true understander,
Who kept within sight of his meaning.
    Without understanding,
          The big man
Goes down into darkness, forgotten.
    That man's dumb as a dog,
    With nothing more said.

God, God of Gods
(No other here pink morning peaks
The violet quench of darkness falling
Hiss into the sea) divided
Portions at the family supper:

To some:
    I God am God I
  Need no roast lamb smoke
  In nostrils shifting guilt
    From sheep to goats,
    Enforced confessions.
  What I know you can't know,
Would not tell you, were I hungry.
    I own all.
Does God chew steak, drink goat blood?
    Praise, keep the law,
    And know not need.

To others:
    Lip service, fingers
  Crossed behind your back,
    Thieves, cheaters,
False oath swearing tale bearers:
    Am I dumb?
    Is this my image?
  I will smash your faces in
The mirror you make up to, gazing
    Into shallow pools,
      And there you'll sink.

Think, in time all will
Take the cup, and drink.

51   Oratory

Like a mother bear her shapeless newborn,
Lick me into cub, O Lord — my proper shape:
I'd rather turn out true than clever, steeped
In arcane brews intent on power,
Wanting wisdom. Make me water
Melted from the summer glacier, run off
Over crushed bone, gravel, spilled
From the stone lip into singing pools.

The sound of water's better than the roar
Of animals burnt on an altar: the broken

Heartfelt not heart's blood makes sacrifice
Acceptable to God, which freshens Zion.

52   *Directly*

Still boasting, mister taking care of number one?
(That sharp-tongued artist of the two-edged shaves
His mustache when he licks his upper lip.)

Kiss off what you've piled up by sacrificing
To your pot, what lies have gotten. Cracks
Will swallow down your house and children whole.

And me? I pluck ripe olives from the garden hedge,
Trusting the invisible supports
My next step, although the earth's crust's hollow.

61

∞

*The
Mountain
Sound*

53 *The Fool Says to Himself*

The fool says to himself, What God?
And takes, and breaks his word, and does
No good, no, none, not anyone. Such rot
In fruit would sicken flies.

God peered down through his window
In the sky, to see his children
At their lives, the men and women,
To find if even one still tried to know

Life and good from death and evil,
But they'd all gone back to witches'
Days, and gold greed blood haphazard couples
And no one knows, does, good, or teaches.

Don't they have an inkling of their doing,
Dying without shame and chewing
Up the people (who would, could they, love
The lore) like bakers' crusty loaves?

The bad have not called God by any name, not even
When the fear came on them, fear that floats
Like bone ash puffed by chimneys in the air, spouts
Of naked ignorance despised shamed by no God.

If only someone would save us from
The blind, our selves, the bloated, come
He from Jerusalem or nearer home

To sunder what has hindered us
From freedom and from happiness,
Then Israel, who wrestled, shall rejoice.

54 Hideaway

Hear, save me,
In your name,
By your strength,
(My soul calls)
From those who know
Nothing, nor you.

It helps me,
Supports me,
Abashing the bad ones.
Praise God
For crushing them
Now, in my lifetime.

55   Feint

God, bad enough to listen to the lies
Enemies bandy. My heart skips.
    Fear of death impales me.
Given dove wings, I would fly
Into some empty place, and nest,
And rest, and there ride out the wind.

Scatter them, Lord, crack their lying
Beaks like bricks dropped from a city wall.
Mischief scrawled cold rumors on it,
Gave my name to what they did.

Worse, no enemy defamed me,
No flunkey from the other camp:
One of my own, familiar to my prayers,
My talk, my table. We would walk together.

I trust the words I say to God,
Not time, or size, or numbers.
    Prayers will save me
From confusion and mutation.
But that friend who stretched
His hand against me, speaking
Butter, all the while bent
To shave me with his razor tongue:
Level him like Babel Tower.
I trust that clay man will die young.

    They open up their mouths
To spit, to swallow me, to tear
    Whatever words might dress
My actions in their sight to tatters.
    I say "right," they hiss "left."
The adders hatch, and lurk, and cook.

The chapter in your book where gossip's measured
    Against praise says none can harm me.
    God is for me. What I know
Is written out, and pours like bottled water:
    Spread a wing, Dove, let its shadow
    Drive these basking lizards back
Into their holes. I want to cross the field
Lightly, want to give more than I take.

65

∞

The

Mountain

Sound

57 Intact

My mother told me:
When you come to the end
Of your rope,
Tie a knot, and hang on.
The knot's secure.
I swing on the bow
Arm of a cello,
Bridge with four strings,
Between steel
Towers outlined after sunrise
And their night lights
Blinking yellow,
Green.

They put snakes
Inside a woven basket,
Puff into the reed drone bladder, charm
Deaf adders with their spells
"That worked once, and will work again."
A mother
Lion licking afterbirth
Is likelier to purr for them, that pack
Of jackals giving tongue.
Extinct them,
Make them unborn, pull their teeth,
And I will count it as a victory
For those who go unwashed
In blood, for sense,
For feeling there's an order.

67

∞

The
Mountain
Sound

59 Mutts

Outside, dogs who worship
Human masters howl against me,
Want to taste my blood, to take
My place. At night the starving pack
Fights, lifts its leg upon my gate,
Pants, drools, and snarls curses at me,
Certain God won't hear, or care.

Some mockers make a butt of innocence,
But cannot take a joke at their expense:
Having sucked their way into the seat,
They fear, perhaps, a loss of dignity
Should one pull back the chair. Take off
The table, Lord, show their bare laps.

After dark the pack sniffs over trash heaps
For scrap meat; dawn finds them restless,
Snappish. Daylight, I am calm
    Inside my fortress.

60   Another Toast

O God, the cup
You pass to us
Is crazed, is cracked.
We drink it up.

God said, On earth
I'll rest my sandal.
Jordan is my
Fingerbowl,
Zion's sky
An empty doorway
To my city.

We said, But dip
And we will sip, Lord.
Always angry?
Always praised.

69

∞

*The
Mountain
Sound*

61   Unstrung

Low tide, land's end, terns
Pluck morsels from the seabed.
Turn me out, God, let me be
Ocean bottom, dune, a looming rock:
Something larger, higher than
That world contracted in my heart.
I want to live a long time, singing
Songs that mean and, saying, do.

∽

62   Intent

I set my heart on finding
　　How the world worked,
Not the gossip business, old
Saws tried and true enough,
　　But mountain bolts
　　Of holy holy
Sacred flame low steady
Shimmers in the desert
　　Haze unspoken
　　Word a serpent
Biting tail in mouth
　　Unbroken circle
Keep the great beyond:

Little boys are vain.
They pick on one another,
　　Check the mirror.
The grown-up wise tell lies
　　About their powers.
Both are lighter than they seem.
Don't say, "I have done nothing."
God spoke twice:
　　"Strength comes from me,"
And,
　　"To each according
　　　　To his deeds."

71

∞

The
Mountain
Sound

63 Canopy

I wanted to see God more than I wanted
Water in the desert, more than power
Over others, so I watched the night sky
Drinking deep cold milky spray.
Next day I stretched out on the couch,
Remembering the nightwatch:
"Distances inside me go
Deeper than a planet's shadow
On the outer rings. Catch hold."
But set my enemies beneath
Your notice, feed them to the dogs
That howl all night, hungry, outside
City walls. Let me sing more.
Stop the liars' mouths with dirt.

Plots afoot.
They press a button.
Barbs fly from nowhere.
Tracks well covered. No ends dangle
Loose, for clues. Perfection.

Great Detective!
Who escapes deduction?
Not the mouthpiece chopping
Logic, who'll have to hear his heart
Attacked. That cheers me up.

73

∽

The
Mountain
Sound

65 Noised

We wait for you, Lord,
    Even here.
Choose someone of us,
    Let him near
You, brave enough to hear
    Your answer.
Winter gales spew oceans
    Of salt rain.
Mountain faces crumble, scree
    Banks streams.
Rivers muddied glide into the sea,
    Mouths open.
We hear the oceans inside
    Seashells, see
Whole cities in a puddle,
    Taste the air.
Your far stars blink in colors,
    Freak the jet.
A year breathes out and in.
    When rocks
Seem soft, the air has edges:
    All living
Shout your praises, or doubting
    Softly sing.

What made all the earth has been
Forgotten even by the ones disposed to know.
Perhaps a list of what was done for Jacob's children helps:
The Red Sea parted, they crossed dry shod,
Following the smoke and fire pillar placed before them.
Stranger prophets could not curse them.
Basic appetites would test them, thirst and hunger
Make them falter, long for Egypt's slave abundance.
Forty years a generation wandered looking backward,
    disappeared.

75

∞

I appear before the book God gave to Moses
With full hands, with promises made when
I could not know I would be able, kept:
The ox, the goat, the lamb, the song of praise.
God heard the music of my heart. I leapt.

The
Mountain
Sound

67   Sow?

If dust stays dry, and clouds bring only wind,
Then people dread the sunrise. Morning hymns
Sound hollow. Not for us. We follow seed
With hope and harvest grain with thanks. God
Made fields to produce. God led us, when
We could not remember what believing was,
With promised land, and fed us in the waste.

∞

Sunrise, the fog fibers trail on breezes
With woodsmoke, cold wax melts, mute fear visions vanish.
But we will get up, will recite a long song:

Tall clouds bank the highway, the blue one God travels,
Over the lonely hearts' home, where we willing dance
Madly to old tunes piped in from the wasteland.

Once children went walking on thorns in the desert
Through earthquake and droughtland. They carried no bottle.
Dew fed their hunger, and washed them, refreshed them

As now we hope rain falls to water the grainfields,
To green up our grazing lands, pastures, the orchards
Of fruit hanging ripe, falling, peels on fire.

Doves wheel, gulls mew, feathers turned yellow
In sunlight so deep that its shadows are snowcaps
On white mountain peaks where the wind wails baldly,
Down pine forest foothills of moss and soft boulders.

A blessing, the day we were led out of Egypt.
Hot snakes gasped, the sea, silenced, bowed back before us:
Egyptians and Canaanites, dog food and fish bait.

Our small children danced to the names of their enemies:
First came the singers, then instruments, drummer girls
Marked time for merchants, slaves, priests, scholars, princes:

77

⮞⮜

The
Mountain
Sound

Our youngest will lead us, will rebuild Jerusalem,
Level the bramble bush, free us, retrieve us
However we're scattered.

Look at the sky. It speaks if you have an ear.
What could contain the blue? Eyes cannot find its end.
Praise as we're able to, maker of atoms, the actor upon us
Whose presence we walk through.

69   Sinking

Sucked down slowly, so I know
My feet will not touch bottom.
Soupy sand creeps past my neck,
My chin. Help. God,
If I open my dry mouth,
Muck will ooze in.
I slipped among the ones
Who love not, liars, fakers,
Thieves, who feed on others'
Misery, who smile and shake
Hands underneath the table.
You do not deal with them
As you have dealt with me,
Though I wore hopsack
To their satin, though
I fasted at their feast,
The butt of drunken
Songs they tooted.
I composed you psalms.

So save me now, show
Mercy without pity.
Answer, blush
From my disgrace,
As though you did not know it.
Turn the mockers' tables
Into settings they can't rise from,
No relief despite the pressure
Built between their jellied thighs

And buttocks, blind them, blister
Ulcers, gut too weak to stand,
Then make them listen to repeated
Stories of the good
Grown rich again.

                    Though incense
Raise a scented column in the sky,
Though long-horned bulls die
On the altar, the knife's work
Is not so pleasant as a song,
The work of life. God hears them
With the sun, moon, stars, earth, sea, and air:
What stirs inside them stirs us.
God save us then, make good
Our losses which shook everything
But what we knew, our memories
Of Zion, when we will return.

70 Quickly

Hurry, carry me away
From those who wish me ill and hurt.
Give them confusion for dessert.
Stump them with flusters as they go
    "Tsk, tsk."
Let all who look outside themselves
Make happy choices, bless their chances:
But I have nothing, now, so help me
    God, do not delay.

81

∞

The
Mountain
Sound

71   Old

Closer to the end, I always trusted
Life continues, though at times
The outlaw bands surrounded me
On horseback in the open plains,
Fired repeated shots
And no rock, no cave, no cliff nor cover near.
Since childhood, I have survived
Their godforsaken consultations,
A young man born to rule
Himself, and others. Now white hair
Wisps, my grip slack on the walking stick,
And people when they look at all
See baggy suit, large knuckles folded
One upon the other, don't quite catch
The name, the choice that made me
What I am.
       I lift my head up
From the table doze. Late afternoon
In winter sunlight floods our benches
Anchored to the traffic islands.
My companions ply their canes,
Beat time while sitting, but I sing
Because I'm able: God
       Of Israel, still twang
     The evening string, my soul
Caught sweetly in the longer shadows:
Darkness swallows up confusion
Raking gravel smooth around the ruin.

Give this child judgment, and more children
    So that he, and they, can govern
One another, face-to-face, like Moses talking
    To the well-spring wished
That all the offspring might be prophets.
    That mountain shadow
Lengthened in the wilderness. It touched
    Our cities, made the far
Ends of the earth, lands beyond the sea
    Remember what life might be
Like, if wanting didn't make us bow to idols,
    Power, money, safety, famous
For a time, then ground and scattered by a wind.
    If not this one, let someone
Come and lead us to ourselves. We lift our hand
    To fend the needless blow,
Will feed the needy then. We show the blossom,
    Trunk, limb, fruit, sow
Grain, and knead the bread. We think the sunlight
    Gold on the west wall
Is afternoon. Let us know more than can be said.

83

∞

The
Mountain
Sound

Book Three NOT YOU AND
NOT THOSE THINGS

～ Psalms 73–89

73   As If

Here's a picture of the bad ones I once envied:

Everything came easily: they did not need
To work to make their living, want
A catchy line, an angle to find lovers or companions
At the dining table: tan and fit from laps and basking
Poolside, they order drinks and gaze at the deep sky,
Chuckle at the devil, protest unjust god:
Superstitions meant for dimlit losers.
They eat the land bare, suck the ocean
Dry as though they had it in their goblet, tall
And frosted, with their tongues' tips swish
Strong currents of the deep.
                              If I painted
Such a picture for you once, just feeling
Without understanding that I envied
Not another person but a creature of my dreams,
Then my mind would curdle, heart dry up,
And I'd have been the dream beast I invented.
But the real touched me, cool and smooth,
Taught me to be able to have everything,
Need nothing, like the names of things
That are not you and are not those things
Either, in a picture story song.

87

∞

Not You
and Not
Those
Things

74 Deafened

Why always angry, God? Why smoke against us and inhale
    Sacrifices? Zion's rubble. Temple hacked
To splinters, they burn children with their teachers.
    No sign, no prophet here to read
A dream or point to ashes' traces of some promised justice.
    They mock the name that I can't
Speak, and gingerly pluck baubles from the coals.
      Destroy them, Lord.

    Return us. You once crushed
The seven-headed ocean-haunting twisted beast Leviathan
    And fed his brains as manna cake

To children in the desert. You opened springs from rocks,
    You raised silt islands from deep
River beds, and dried them. You set sun and moon, the different
    Bodies of the day and night, you
Flickered lightning bugs in summer garden spaces between trees,
    Made standing puddles glinting ice.
      You taught us, now deliver us
From those who worship templed darkness. Look,
    We blush for you, your name,
Though we are poor, and weak, and strangers roar.

75   *Horn*

I lift up my arms, and watch the earth rise
Above its base self, upon pillars, on praise.
While fools cut sharp deals in the dog teeth of death,
They blow their own horns. Their necks stiffen.

What lifts us up comes from within, without
One false note, or false steps, or deception.
Pour off the good wine; let the bad
Swill the bowl's dregs, get plastered and flushed.

More than sing songs of praise, God,
I'll cut off the horns of their boast in mid toot;
Raise your own horn heads, brass with silvery valves,
Lift the bell full of blue sky and blow.

89

∞

Not You
and Not
Those
Things

76 Then

Israel once saw the law made visible,
Took heart,
Built God's house in Jerusalem.

Armies rained night fire on Zion's mountain.
Terror took them in their sleep.
Sometimes love in sight of danger
Makes an old man angry
90 Wishing for the end of time,
A dry well deeper than the hate of strangers.

∞

Book
Three

77 Shake

Hear me, first of all, when night sweats attack
My sleep with sores, with jitters, pacing. Faces
Haunt me. I play music, hope the fright will pass.

What happened? Am I no more fortune's
Favored singer, dreamer, seer, drenched
In oils, visions, dances? Can the bottomless run dry?

You once stood by Joseph and for Jacob's children held
Pharaoh at arm's length, made water part. Clouds
Streaked day's streaming face. Light nocked its arrow.

When God's foot skips a beat upon the ocean floor
(The ocean that's above us), no one knows or sees
The measure. Time remains to lead us by the hand
    Of a Moses, of an Aaron.

91

∞

Not You
and Not
Those
Things

78 *Crooked*

The past is riddled with old stories
Told by grandparents to children:
Remember how the people came
To be called chosen, and no sooner
Hoped than were forgotten?
                                    God
Reminded Jacob's children's children
Of their nomad fathers' deep confusion:
Who were they? Where did they come from?
How sea water stood like dikes
Against the flood of Pharaoh's army,
How day cloud and night fire made a pillar
Signpost where there was no road,
How bare rock spouted rivers through
The wasteland, and how people spoke
Against what saved them, asked for meat
To go with water, asked for bread,
For table service where there was no table.

God heard them, rumbled heaven open,
Tumbled manna from the sky, threw wheat
For angel cake, sent dust storms stocked
With quail dropped around their tents.
They ate what cravings made them. Full,
They pushed back from the table
And complained. God cut them down.

For all this they believed no more
In providence than in their own days:

Water poured on rock at noon.
Seeing shadows overtake them
They remembered what made mountains
Mumble, staggered by the burden
Of just being's vacant lot.
God remembered flesh was made
Of knowing, life a ripple shortly
Smoothed on doldrum waters. If not
Miracles, why not believe
In plagues? Blood clotted Nile
Swarming flies, frogs, fields rattling
Clouds of grasshoppers and locusts,
Hail-beaten grapevines, frost
Nipped sycamores, sheep and cattle
Lightning spitted, epidemic, last
The first-born of all Egypt
Taken on the dark wing as they slept.

God led his children out of bondage,
Through the sea and into emptiness,
Sat them around the holy mountain,
Read them stony laws, shook out
Nations from the skirting lands
Time promised them, and pitched their tents.

Children, grown to be their fathers,
Praised statues, groves in hillside shrines.
A fair breeze folded Jacob's tents
Among their enemies: no ark,
No promise left, the young men burned
Or butchered, virgins taken without

Not You
and Not
Those
Things

Ceremony, priests erased,
And widows did not mourn at all.

That silence shook the rock awake, and
David, chosen from his pastures, toppled
Giant idols with a sling. He built
A court in Zion. People followed him.
He shepherded the children skillfully.

79 Trespass

Foreigners have broken down the old walls
Of Jerusalem. God's chosen rot
In open places, food for vultures, ravens, jackals.
Their blood became a river through Jerusalem,
Our name a joke, a byword, and a taunt.

How long before you pour down
Wrath upon those who will not hear
You have a name, who ignorant
Burn books and torture learning, forge
Us iron chains and say, "Where is their God?"

A prisoner cannot cry loud or long.
Cramp their mocking hearts, God, seven
Spasms for each curse; for every day, a week.

∞

Not You
and Not
Those
Things

80   Come

Listen, reader of the dreams
Interpreted by Joseph, who led
Israel into Egypt, brought them
Up again: return us to ourselves.

However long it takes to mill,
To knead the sorry flour, our bread
Crumbles and the neighbors jeer.

Return us to ourselves. Why plant
These terraced hills with vineyards,
Cork trees, almonds, olives, cedars,
Willows trailing in the river?

Passing strangers trample down
Thorn hedges, pluck the orchards
Bare. Deer and boar root out

The broken fruit. Can you look down
And not return us to ourselves,
The chosen cutting scorched, uprooted?
O unpronounceable that made us,

Make us strong again. We know
There is no going back.
Return us to ourselves.

81   Open

What the God of Jacob said through Joseph, we sing
In a psalm, accompanied by tambourine and shepherd's harp.
 New moon, full moon, blow the horn of Israel
  Again. About the law:

When I sent Joseph down to Egypt
 (Strange tongues spoken there)
I took his brothers off his shoulders,
 Saved him from the chore pots.
 He called, I answered him
With dreams. I answer you with thunder:
 Split rocks gush bitter water.

 Do not worship strangeness
In yourself or others' glamour:
I led you out of Egypt, and will
 Fill your mouth. Just open
When I speak: but no one listens.

Had they not loved the sound of their own voices,
 Chosen lust, and meat, and hate,
I would have made them masters over all they met,
Would have fed them white bread milled from finest wheat,
 Spread with honey from the rock.

97

≈

*Not You
and Not
Those
Things*

82 Inheritance

Those with heaps of money, made
Or born to it, though they play
With bankers, senators, with generals,
Like gods to mortals, while they
Stroll in knots through crowded halls
Where others bustle, they are judged,
Rejected by what they don't know,
And think because they can command
They are beloved. Not for long.
Time to stand up for the put-upon,
Who must believe the bad do well
Because they would be gods, as I am
Certain all of us are children
Of the Lord, but also humans
Who will die, will fall like rulers
From the high seat to a black hole:
Wake up, judge, the gods decay
And leave the earth for you.

83 Catalogue

Speak now against the nations
Leagued against us, God,
That would erase all trace of Israel:
Edom, Ishmael, Moab and the sons of Hagar;
Byblos, the Amalekites, the Philistines,
Phoenicians and Assyrians, Lot's children:
Crush them like Midian, drive nails
Through their temples like Jael luring Sisera;
Grind their bones for fertilizer, make them —
Kings who thought to seize our grazing lands —
Soft prey for Gideon, who tossed
Their dry husks to the tumble wind:
Be fire to their timber, blow hot
Hurricanes into their eyes until they fall
Flat on their faces when the least of Jacob's
Whispers, once we read your name.

99

∞

Not You
and Not
Those
Things

84 Amiable

Sparrows rant in the ivy walls of a brick courtyard.
Broad eaves shelter swallows. Rain streaks dust
Tracks down windows, overflowing the stone birdbath.
Some puddles are deeper than the towers they reflect.
A crowd of finches stretch their wings, splash,
Chatter. The doorman takes more cheer
From them than from the tenor oboing his scales
Behind a velvet curtain. He also feels the sun
Beam through the damp lens more directly,
    And his head is covered.

100

85 Willing

God once smiled on Israel,
Returned them from captivity,
    Forgotten and forgiven.
Now think of us, let us remember
More than anger, more than children
    Heaped before their fathers.
Speak us peace, and all who are not
Fools must listen. Blow one kiss
    And dandelions, truth
Will sprout through cracking sidewalks, wild
Puffballs, fierce and multiplying.
    The second kiss brings rain.

101

∞

*Not You
and Not
Those
Things*

Listen, God, I need
You, hear me.
    Cheer me
In this darkness.
Give me back
(My soul is ready
Now to leave me)
Any answer.
I don't question
You believe me.
Teach me trust
In the returning
Promise, shame
My enemies
In public, enter
My heart in your
Book of splendors.

87 Born

The sky rests on the mountains
Like a house on its foundation;
God has blessed the doors of our houses
More than any place in any other city:
A gorgeous name and musical, Jerusalem.

You know me as a man from maybe Rahab, Babylon;
Another harks from Tyre, Ethiopia, or calls
Philistia his birthplace; but to be born in Zion
Is a blessing, is to be born inside the holy city.
It counts, by all accounts, to pray, Jerusalem.

My mother, home of singers
And strummers on the living strings:
All there, and there my being springs.

103

∽

*Not You
and Not
Those
Things*

88 Stacks

I cry and cry, so down I can't get out of bed.
My bedroom floor yawns like a grave
Where, free, the dead stack, sunk below.
The family waves good-bye, remembering.
Friends turn aside, look past my shoulder.
I no longer leave the house,
I have no face to show the world,
And I still call to you, and wonder
Can the dead stop in their tracks, amazed,
And stand up cheering what you do?
What good is kindness to the pit,
Or accuracy in oblivion?
          And yet I cry: I clutch
The hem of morning. You ignore me.
Young and ignorant, I suffered
Fears flocked in my face like crows
At carrion, and I am not alone:
All I have known have done
The quick dissolve, and enter darkness.

89   Mask

I made love to the sky,
To steady stars, its milky blurs:
Day's the night's mask worn for us.
We don't live by starlight's frozen
Sequined curtain never opened.

Some have chosen to believe
What can't be certain: others made
God vanish in a flood of wordy bargains,
Filled with reasons there's no justice.
Comparisons can't break the sea surge.

What newborn's larger than its mother?
Planets cooled from eddied gases,
Thought's a bubble. Home, our habit
Was to listen for some inkling
What the sky meant. And it spoke once:

"I poured oil on the child's head
Who sang to me, not out of need,
Of generations grown from seed,
Tall cedars axes will not cut down,
Shelter from the moth, the flame:

"The sea in one hand, Jordan
In the other, he will be both sweet
And salty to the taste, to those
Who love, or hate, and he shall call me
Father, maker of the mountains,

"Shaker of the world to come,
And I will place him first
Among the living always. He will
Live fulfilled, when his cold bones
Know he's dying, that his son's sons'

Sons will sit in splendor for an hour
Of their day in heaven. Broken laws
I punish, but not broken hearts.
This child's name will last as long,
No, longer than the sun and moon."

Children never listen.
Singsong taunts
And pointed fingers.
What God greater?
Who's your father?

How much longer must we take it?
Is life really hollow nothing?
We are born, we live, we die,
But to live out death in life?
Not to love even myself?

Promise me like yesterday
You told the child
You would love him always.
Tell me now they pour down
Insults, oil on my head.

Book Four WHERE WE HAVE
ALWAYS LIVED

∾ Psalms 90–106

Lord, where we have always lived
Before the earth and sun were born,
You made us children of destruction
And ask us to return again, return
Although an eye blinks and a thousand
Years pass, though the night watch hours
Creep crawl to eternity. Days crest
Past on the sweeping flood, sleep
To the sleepless, no sooner grown then mown
Grass, clippings blown across the walk.
Your anger wind time swallows up
Our secrets, whistles through our faults,
Our faces masks worn in a tale
Seventy or eighty years (that's
For the lucky) told in work and tears.
How strong's the wind? More than we fear.
So teach us how to weigh a day,
To wear the burden of a heart.
Because we do not know how long
Before we must return, Lord,
Damp the dust with small rain, shade
The strong sun behind towered clouds
Sometimes, so that our children know
A dappled place much like our fathers had,
But happy, not the evil we have learned
To handle, greedy factories of hate,
And let some part of what we've made last
Touch upon you, that part
A heart or hand has made.

109

∞

Where
We Have
Always
Lived

91 Address

Live sheltered by the shadow of the highest
    Mountain and remember
When you walked through quicksand,
Plagues passed over other doorsills in the dark,
Days when arrow swarms pursued and thousands fell
    Around you, and you stood, unmarked.
As you saw the latter parts of splendor pass before you,
Watch the bad ones' lives become their punishment.

110
    Angels guard you, guide your steps
      Down curbs through heavy traffic.

Book
Four
Because one called out the unspoken name
    I answer cries with laughter,
      Turn labor into honors,
Teach the flavor of cold water.
    He will live a long time
      And be thought of later.

Thank you. I love
To sing at first light,
Pluck a gut string
In the watches of the night:
A little song, with rocks
And sea, and sky, without
Confusion of the parts.

Rocks sink. The sea is deep.
It holds the sky's dear
Face, the sun and moon
Also. Life started here.
Fools don't believe
This, think the waters
Tame and sounded,
Something with a name.

I heard music, foghorns
Over jetties, smelled
Sap from fresh-cut cedar
Trees that grew straight
Up the mountain slopes
Of Lebanon. Let me grow
Old, let my sap run.

111

∞

Where
We Have
Always
Lived

93 Attention

The ruler wrapped on earth and sky
Measures the world, that fixed
Place where people live and hear
The heartbeat ocean break
Waves up limestone cliffs, blue air,
And know God dwarfs the sound
Of tidal bores. Hard to unravel
Knots in a high gale, or silent
Calm when sun bears down, so we live
Here content to think we know yet may
Not say your real name forever.

Up, up, and show yourself
The judge of people doing what they want,
   Saying what they will and damn
The consequences. "Nothing follows, meaning's
     Deader than the children
   Crushed beneath our jackboot heel.
    Let them whimper. God
Is not, is far away, and does not care."

Some never learn. Can one who planted
Ears of corn not hear the zephyr rustle
   In the stalks, who made the sun's eye
Flare not see the shadow you cast here?
The scatterer of nations not disperse
Your atoms? Is the teacher unprepared?
    God knows how thought gets mangled.
So law was given Moses to untangle
Ignorance and impulse, love and fear
   Of what comes after, for a snare.

Had I not heard from life beyond my silence,
I'd have slipped into the crowd unseen
And died without desire comforted.
    Too neat, my Lord? You taught me
Safety in disorder, and the pleasure
   Of imagining that justice
Crushes glinting evil to gray powder.

113

∞

Where
We Have
Always
Lived

95 Waste

The rock we stand on is the rock
We sing to: deep as wellshafts
High as glacier tops: the land
We live on and the ocean smaller
Only than the sky that rests inside
Its cup:
      A heart is harder
Than the wilderness our fathers
Wandered, proof that they were
Human, bitter like the aftertaste
Of water in a mouth turned forty
That has never kissed except
In lust, or rage, or envy, after
Wanting, wanting, and no rest.

New moon, new song:
Day short, night long.
Break sea, roar winds:
One God, more minds.
Stars blink. Suns cool.
Tongues twist. Souls rule.
Smoke's sweet. Song doubts.
Times dance. Rain spouts.

Lose hope. Sow seed.
Cast bells. Ring true.
Not want, just need.
First frost. Late dew.

115

∽

Where
We Have
Always
Lived

97 *Original*

I saw a picture of the earth afloat
In space: a solar marble, cloud
Veins in blue ore, oceans studded
With green islands, continental
Rust, capped, footed by iced poles:
Water-swollen mountain glaciers
Melted in the sun's wax candle.
What chains this jewel hung

On vacuum's throat? Who knows
The name, could show a sliver
Of that shattered beaker (left
Behind when all the other shards
Swept back to nothingness) was
Creation's germ, and not be pierced
So deeply no blood flowed? Be glad
We're small, be glad no one can tell
What happens next and no returning.
Only one returns those promises
Substantial as the sands our fathers
Sifted through their fingers
For us, moments when their hearts
Felt easy, and they did not boast.

98 Hmm

Sing a new song at the new moon,
The old sky, a sickle for harvesting
All we remember. Our versions

Might last long as drumbeats
And footfalls. The left hand stops
Frets and the right strums in tempo.

Clouds dance with conductors.
And thunder claps. Mountains peak.
Waving, the wind clears its throat.

117

∞

Where
We Have
Always
Lived

99   Wholly

An avalanche shakes clots
Of peak into the passes,
Thunder under cloud.

A cloudy pillar talked to Moses.
Moses spoke to Aaron. Samuel
Heard his name called after bedtime,

Learned to call upon the Lord.
They worshipped what almost
Forgave them, then did, finally.

Festival

It helps to make a lot of noise
When on the earth. We did not,
Were modest, too, until God made us
Enter squally bawling thank-yous
In our lifetime, children's children.

119

∞

Where
We Have
Always
Lived

101 *Visit*

Lord, I can only sing
What my senses show,
Unless it come to me
From you. So when?

I never worshipped pictures,
Cultivated adders by detracting others,
Said what one could never know.
I cut their puffs off in mid-sentence.

120

The sky is blue but blank.
Fire crackles in the leaves.
Wood smoke curls to heaven.
I do not hanker for dry reeds,
No pelican with empty bill blown inland,
An owl in daylight far from rafters:
One sparrow perched on the roof ridge,
Crow flocks circle me with caws.
They snatch my crumbs, and no one
Drives them off. My days have gone
To creeping shadows, brown
Grass waiting for the sickle.
But you, you last, you live
For children of the since departed.
You will help them later,
Because the stones and dust
Of foreign places became their pleasure,
Because they have remembered how
To pray, to say what's in their hearts,
Your name. This will be written
To their children, and the lined-up
To be born will sing your praise:
Who can see from a great height
Into the earth and hear the groans:
Release time's hostage passion poisoned:
Crowds dying whispering "Jerusalem."

I walked, I weakened, breath got short:
I said, Not now, Lord, in the middle

121

∞

Where
We Have
Always
Lived

Of these days born and done
Beyond the rim of time where earth
First met the sun and moonlight sky:
Stars also fall out of their frame,
A canvas hung in weather tatters,
Then's exchanged for new. But you
Don't change, don't track the way
The spokeless years do. You protect
Your children, and their children
Do go on.

∞

My soul remembers but does not
Know how to say the name:
That one forgives without forgetting,
Draws me living from the pit again,
Rings changes, stays the same.

A burning bush made Moses know
Himself, while Israel discovered
Anger does not last forever,
Nor do crimes against each other.
We are small, have need to measure.

The distance from the top of living
Heaven to the bone cold deep of time
Beggars numbers, but allows no space
For what we call our God inside
There, even by comparison.

That made us clay from dust,
Our days like grass, our pleasures wild
Flowers blown by passing breezes:
Come and gone, we know ourselves
No longer, and are known no more.

The children's children heard of days
Always returning, so they hope to learn
From life, and good, and death and evil.
They set a ruler in the sky, to measure
Water leaked between their fingers.

Tonight the sky's a slate cleared for some word:
Meteors, star spray, and falling messengers.

123

∾

Where
We Have
Always
Lived

Bless the pitcher of the sky's light tent
    (Winds are tentpoles, clouds stays),
Who draws the curtains, sends out messengers:
    Old stars chilling distances;
The rising sun burns puddles hung with rope
    Mists on the changing earth.
. Bless the layer of the rock foundation,
    Raiser of the great divides,
Where rivers fork to east or west, in beds,
    And find sea level in the end,
And rise again. Fresh springs, rock wells quench
    All thirsts that walk, or fly, or set
Seed, bud, green up and flower fruit: wine
    Grapes to ease the heart; fat olives,
Herbs and cereal grasses to make bread.
    Sap rises in the junipers
Of Lebanon: storks nest there. In cliff clefts
    Mountain goats hopscotch and butt.
The moon marks fallow plowing sowing harvest
    Seasons, and the sun sets. Nights,
Horned owls hunt for mice, and lions roar
    At starlight for large prey. Dawn,
Raptors flap or slip back to the den,
    Leaving day work to the human
Makers of their own invented prizes.
    Ocean — broad and sometimes taller
Than the headland, silver shadow creatures
    Glide through transparent density,
Slip underneath the keel like lives of people

124

∞

Book

Four

Only known as chthonic rumor —
Floats Leviathan, fed on krill and plankton,
    The largest on the smallest, full.
Creation grazes from your open hand:
    God, never turn away.
Without the breath, all's clay, and dead.
    Love answers fear. Earth's
Greater than what's known. What's known
    Exceeds what's said.
So touch the mountains with your smoking finger.
    I'll chant praises of my being
Here long as I can. The ignorant,
    Their darkness, disappear.

125

∞

Where
We Have
Always
Lived

105 Pasture

A cold wind in the treetops:

Remembering put words to it:

How Abraham and Jacob chose
To listen, wrestled with the first
Belief: that earth was given to us
When there were a few of us
So we might know where
We came from, and could sing again
The promise made to Abraham,
Sworn over prostrate Isaac, pledged
To Jacob at the draw: All yours.

For that small tribe, strange kings
Turned impotent, for them the dreamer
Sold ahead to slavery, for them
The harvests failed. Joseph, shackled,
From his prison read the glyphic
Pharaoh's dreams as living speech;
Named steward to the land, he
Brought Israel to Egypt. There
They fed. The children multiplied.
Egyptians played them false.

For them, the one thread that connects
Beginning to the end yet has none, sent
Moses and Aaron, serpents, blood
For Nile water, frogs on bedsheets, swarming

Flies, mosquitoes, hail, lightning flattened
Fields blighted orchards vineyards: locusts
Blanketed the gardens, God
Struck down all Egypt's firstborn
For them, leaving Egypt weeping
At their backs, and spread a cloud above them
To keep off the sun. A pillared fire
Burned at night. For them, live quails,
Bread from stone-ground wheat,
For them sweet water gushed between the rocks.

∽

So God remembered all his promises
To Abraham, and led his chosen
People singing Hebrew out of exile   *Where*
Freely as wind passes through tall trees: *We Have*
The land was theirs as long as they remembered   *Always*
How the story goes, and kept the law.   *Lived*

Praise returns
This people to the home they left
For foreign places, flavors rolled
Upon the tongue, flat bread
Broken at a stranger's table.

We are children of the fathers
Who forgot what led them up
From Egypt, made the reed sea
Part for them, a sandy causeway
Through the gulf. When water
Buried Pharaoh's army
They believed, but only
For a little while: hunger
Made them whine, made quail
Drop from clouds and water
Split bare rock. God fed them,
Yet their souls were thin,
Transparent: envy bucked
At Moses, Aaron: the earth
Cracked and swallowed Dathan.
They cast a bull of molten gold
At Horeb, as a thing to hang
Religion on. They could not bear
The inexplicable performed
By namelessness. Though Moses
Stood between them and the blast
Of wonder, they would live
Their days out seeing waste,

No land of promises fulfilled.
They grumbled in their tents.
On their account their children's
Children's children would be
Captives forced to eat the leavings
Of the dead. Plague ate them hungry,
Turned on Phinehas' spit. Moses,
Stung beside the well of bitter
Waters, let his anger slip.
These fathers lived with strangers,
Married idol lovers, sacrificed
Their babies to the beaks of Canaan,
Coupled every way they could
Imagine. Fortune left them
To be ruled by hatred.
At times some rose to show them
Back to their own selves
And laws, and did, until
Forgetting overtook them.
Yet when a heart, a child cries
Out to the dark, the cry is heard,
And people think about returning.

Gather us together, Lord,
Captives scattered among strangers,
Lead us back, for we remember
Promises and praise.

∞

Where
We Have
Always
Lived

Book Five RETURN. PROMISE.

∽ Psalms 107–150

Receipt

Always returning to the promise, I remember
Some few kept in mind what they had seen
Of parted sea, of wasteland nurture, law.
Wandering the wilderness, they cried out
To God, to their confusion, and were heard.
Their children founded places, and were fed.

So later generations fill their mouths with praises:
Proud minds humbled clang on dentless shells
Of greed, of grief, of gorgeous meditations
In the captive darkness, until, light gone,
They thought that death was freedom.

So later generations fill their mouths with praises:
Prisoners of self, good taste, they found no food
To like, and did not eat, and would have died
Had they not eased the grip on their own throats
And let slip bread and water past their lips.

So later generations fill their mouths with praises:
A sailor's business is the ocean. On his watch
He peered into the abyss: wind twisted masts
Like paper, breakers boiled yellow, rigging
Crackled with drowned souls. The compass spun.

So later generations fill their mouths with praises:
It's possible to die from too much skill,
And possible to live not knowing how
The storm blew, how merchant port was found.
It's possible to live and never once be calm.

133

∽

Return.
Promise.

So later generations fill their mouths with praises:
How people settled cities, planted vineyards,
Sowed grain in fields, covered grazing lands.

So the story keeps returning, of great armies
Lost in deserts, of the small made splendid,
Blessed with family and flocks, of the wicked
Choking on their empty language, hands clapping
Shut the mouth. Some parts return to mind.
A wise one sees things, and may understand them.

I fixed my heart by singing every morning to my harp,
To what returns an answer, to chance questions:

God said:
   I change the earth
Like people change their clothing before battle:
I measured Shechem for a boot: It didn't fit.
I put on Gilead, Manasseh, wore Ephraim
As my helmet, took Judah as my swagger stick.
I wash my hands of Moab. Edom is my bootjack.
   I humble Philistines.

Who will climb the wall first? Who will open Edom?
God knows. When we win, we say that God is with us.
War means death comes only from another's hand.

135

∞

Return.
Promise.

A pack of liars, spitting adders, sometime
Friends accused me of my prayers,
Hauled me to court, and thought
Because their purchased justice heard
The case, that I was caught.
Orchestrated charges' clamor could not drown
The oath I muttered in God's ear.
God is not deaf to truth, can tell

Good judgment from a smear.
I said: Lord,
        Is truth auctioned to the highest
Bidder? Make the devil court's attorney
For this kangaroo judge when he comes
Before you. String his bartered sentences
Through nose-rings. Hale him living
Out of office. Let his life be short,
His widow laugh, then turn a hag,
A char, his orphan children cruise
City streets for bread. Let tax men
Reappraise him, creditors foreclose.
Hold his father's greed against him.
Gratify his mother's lust with strangers,
By an open window in full view of neighbors.
Crush his name to powder, rub away
His chalk. This man brought innocence
To market, has earned hatred.
He wears lies as his robe of justice,
As a tiger skin, so cinch the sash,
Turn blood to water, bone to wax.

Pay back my loveless friends
One hundredfold in coin struck
By themselves, and loaned, and spent.
Not for my sake but because
Your name can slow the reaching
Shadows of an afternoon, make
The full sun halt and blaze for me,
My enemies' near bygone watchword
Hardly worth a taunt.
                            Show your hand,
Lord, make them fear you   137
     And an old man's verse.

                                                     ∽

                                              Return.
                                              Promise.

110 Unusually

God said: Sit down.
Use your enemy's back
For a chair, for a hassock.
Read him several chapters
From your book of successes.

Dew beads on glazed tile.
Days, streets are dusty and heaped
With their bodies. You pause
At the streambed, bend, drink
From an eddy, look up.

Thanks to the maker of the
Infinite, heaped particles, of
Memory, where time —
Escaping even as we watch a rock
Slide rumble down the distant
Mountain face — that groaning
Axle of eternity, spoke of the wheel
Knowing and forgetting. Law
Enacted teaches pity wastes itself.
Roaring dies. Whispered praise endures.

139

∞

Return.
Promise.

112 *Clenched*

Happily, one listens to what's written
About right and wrong.
Light sometimes takes too long to come.
Law does not always side with good.
Enough a person's kind and generous,
Loves fairness more than gain or show.
Ugly, deafened, greedy slandermongers
Jeer, jaw, juggle for the upper hand.
Averse to tricks, the decent one is happy.
His haters' teeth grind even when asleep.

140

∽

Before

The work is never done.
Sunset, sunrise, sky
A high chair spilling
Light crumbs on the floor.
As before, we sweep them
Into heaps, find families
Where once the barren
Wasted time like water
And a mother bears.

141

∞

Return.
Promise.

114   Exit

When Israel went up from Egypt,
A house in a house of no law with strange language,
  The land filled its promise to Jacob.
The sea saw the children on foot and drew back.
  Jordan turned aside.
Boulders skipped down mountainsides like rams
  Jump, like spring lambs.

What quailed the sea so it fled?
    What shunted Jordan?
  Skipped the mountainside?
The presence, God, which makes land pitch
  Made rock melt into standing pools,
    Cliffs spout fountains.

115   *For Why*

Not for our sake, but so strangers will not say
    Where is god?
In the sky? does he listen? then polish
    Their bumpers and crystal,
And go right on braying, and looking not seeing:
    These hummers with tin ears, they
Wrinkle their noses, grope hard under covers,
    And stumble, and cry out:
They are what they worship, and fashion, and trust.   *143*

    Admit what you can't know,
    And can't see, and grow up   *Return.*
To fear it. Grow rich and old, less   *Promise.*
Than the maker of earth and sky,
    Gifts to the living. Give
Life. For what good do the dead do?
    Can they worship, sing praises?
    For as long as you can, live
    And praise, live and praise.

For once when I cried out somebody listened:
God took my complaint for a song
Belted at the top of my lungs
In a shower of troubles, good
Even if off key. Surrounded by death
Loving liars, by fires banked inside
My nature, I stumbled over simple things:
A shoe untied, the pillow never smooth,
A night cough, hum of strangers' tires.

The gift has been given. So, low but alive,
I said what I believed: that greed succeeds
Where grace cannot, that one idea can kill
A world of simple pleasures, cup and spoon.
Stir them. Don't speak quickly, savor
The hot cider, candied ginger on the tongue,
Heavy cloud shrugged off my shoulders.
I promise to be more than one of those
(What, still alive? He lived? He died?) who never
Show their heart or read the lips of mumblers
In the public record: I call upon the Lord,
Am called upon to praise in easy words:
A truth should come out plain and make good sense,
So truth will find a friendly audience.

117 Either

Lord,
All living
Utter praises:
Dead ones don't.

Or:

Heaven covers
Yesterday with
Morning, always:
Now praise.

145

∞

Return.
Promise.

118 *Erected*

Thank goodness just one god always returning.
Let children learn to say, "Always returning."
Let those who lead thought say, "Always returning."
Let those who've seen fear say, "Always returning."

    I called from my narrow self:
    The great expanse answered,
Said: If God is for you, what matter
Who hates you. Far better to trust
    Found disorder than tugs
    Of war, others: give up
To the sky, not mean men.

    Surrounded, I cut off
Their shouts in mid-sentence, shaved
Fringes off whatever small point
They boasted: bee swarms and smoke
    Crackling fired thorns, pinky rings,
Squid-sucker foreskins in heaps on the floor.

    A hip-slapper.
Winners' tents pitch, but the fortunate
Dancer chose pebbles, more killing
Than coping stones dropped from a temple wall.
    Shelter's how things fall out;
    Hope is tomorrow's door.

Happy for good from the name I can't say aloud,
Blue hazes wind through the horns of the altar.
Praise for the ornament, heart plays the instrument:
Thank goodness just one god always returning.

A

As though time casts no shadow,
We acted out the letter of the law
   But left the heart behind, as though
The ocean could be stopped, be tied
   In reasons, ropes. The waters mirror
Changing light, the blank expression
   Of a face that makes no error.

B

Born as we are from the breach, and buried
   In the earth, we made tables
Of law cut in stone by your fingertip,
So the pages might crack but the words would not smudge,
   Like our actions, confusion, despair
   Of fixed meaning. Sun's glare blinds
The sailor, yet he hears white breakers
And gulls mew, scents rocks, and knows danger.

C

Call me. I'll answer,
Only a visitor
Here among strangers
Who sit on their benches
And gossip and mutter
And stare at me. Tell me
Your secrets, the law's lore
In plain words, but softly.

D

Do I talk to the earth and the sky?
   Did they answer?

147

∞

Return.

Promise.

Days, they said. Nights, they sung.
    Wonder of wonders.
Liars believe that the world is their willing:
    Dash them down
Now, Lord, like gravity's dancers. I drink
    Understanding, and run off like water.

E

Entering my judging heart
I found a maze, the same
That pleased the five-year-old
    Who threaded through.
Now paintings, merchant hallways
Twist inside me, though I always
Find a window: moonlight, you
    Make it visible.

F

First let us walk without worry:
If kindness will come, do I need
To answer the taunters who never
Doubt newspaper stories, but titter
When I talk, for saying the right
And just thing as you teach it?
Their fat heads suck flattery, but I eat
Your law, food which won't make me thick.

G

Give me rest. Give me hope. Give me
    Rest from hope.
Worn out from watching and wanting

To see the bad
Ground up and blown off like sawdust.
    Going to sleep
I remember your name, waking your law.
    Does it help?

    H
Hear me now, how I swear
From my heart that your
Pity's no help, Lord.
    You promised.
Read your law, didn't I?
Day and night, praising
Leaps without lapse, Lord,
    Your promise.

    I-J
I served your good words to the pork
Hearted liars, who spat them out. Judge them
In their day, with my mouth, by your book.
While jerks joke about money, paper
Bathrooms with floral prints, teach
Me how truth tastes, how work
Puts forth flowers, for only the sick
Once at heart have an inkling.

    K
    Knowledge without guilt
    May not be how you made me,
But the thought of it makes pain
And fear more pointed, makes me

Return.
Promise.

Willing to exhaust my youth
And stand unblushing before crowds
Of those who cannot see or hear even
My heart's truth, much less your own.

L

Longing to hear from you, all night
        I listened
To dark jars the wind socked, eyes bleary:
        I heard

Speeding cars, dogs barking, horns, no hosannas:
        I said
Lies may not kill me: law written larger than life
        Is the Lord's.

M

Made of memory and will
To know, we are the law's
Unlikely servants, clay
Clouds blown across
The earth we're made from:
Some thrown in others' way
So they'll stumble, or become
Less humbly observant.

N

    Now I get it!
Never put down understanding.
    Save God alone,
Nothing else can help you:
    Money, power,

Man or woman, drug or teacher.
    Hungry? Certain
Words taste sweet, will fill, are true.

        O
Opposite
Darkness, when lumps
Click their lamps off,
Grind molars and cry out,
I turn to your text:
Every letter a torch passed
Along generations: run
Over darkness.

Return.

        P
        Put it this way:
    Little as I know of these worlds,
    Much less what words mean, I pour
Out beakers of red wine, olive oil cruses
At those meals called for as I read the law
    As we have written in your book.
    Poor, any reason to ignore a letter
        That won't go away.

Promise.

        Q
Question you, engraver of the law,
Who by the way made mountains, air, and oceans,
Piled idols into heaps left for the ignorant
To pick from, those without the sense to fear
A whisperer whose prophets' hair stands
Straight up when they're called, who speak

With difficulty, know they won't be heard
But hated because they speak your word? Never.

    R

Right as you are, Lord,
Spare me some assurance
That hooters and honkers
Won't prance it forever
In our fallen faces, who took
What your book said was
Proper as truth. Ruin them
Now, Lord. Or let me. I want to.

    S

Soul, can you see how the sky's blue silk scroll,
Read from right to left, studded with alphabet starlight,
Can be studied the way one can drink in a face,
Each flicker and shadow voicing an emotion?
A script streaked with ink stained by tears of ambition,
The play of emotion no insight no knowledge.
I don't know another except for such outbursts.
I look for myself while searching your law.

    T

The gale blew all night, a howler
In the trees. The ocean stood
Up on its legs and walked white-haired
Across the barrier beach. Driftwood houses
Tumbled from their stilts, too near
Land's end to stand long. Moored in sand,
Just sea grass holds the world in place:
Dunes for our nature, words for grass.

U-V

Unless the end comes quickly —
    Poof! No planet —
We'll be forced to understand it as we go.
    Even nothingness won't be
        As we imagined.
Earth's shoulders shrug the mantle, towers
    Built to code careen, consuming
Knowledge from the atoms up: your sentence.

W-X

Weeks pass. The red oak silver maple leaves
    Paint patterns underfoot. And waffle.
Green earth cools. Will winter ever come?
    Can sky break mountain fog at ten,
Icicles draped across my lips and lashes?
    Whether birth and death the weavers
Ever finish up the rug to cover us, or not,
    Your law stays. We go. X marks the spot.

153

∞

Return.

Promise.

Y-Z

Yet again I called out, and you heard me:
After crowds dispersed, after keepers
Swept up, locked, and left for home, I sang
    Another solo for the Lord
        Alone.
Yes, I remember yesterday, one
Yellow wort in bloom next to the gate.
Zealous without meaning to be, jealous.

120   *Preyers*

I called out to the one who heard me say,
Save me from the plausible liars.
What can be said to a twister of truth, someone
Who preys upon trust, who mints coin from desire?
Bludgeon the bastards with bricks and bats, fire
Them, forbid them to sit on a bench in the sun.
No matter what I say, they contradict it. I say,
Peace, my soul wants peace. But they say, War.

154

∞

121 *Echo*

I look to the hills and hear thunder rolls,
Eternity's wheel
Across highway and foot track:
Who could sleep
In broad daylight or moonlight,
At home or abroad?
God's the great keeper of people
Awake, a keeper
    From evil, forever.

155

∞

Return.
Promise.

My heart danced when they said, Go in:
I stood inside the doorway to Jerusalem:
Jerusalem, the city of the Lord of all

Creation, ruler of the law, of people
Speaking heart to heart, where dream, word, thought,
Justice, judgment, thanks, and praise

Agree, where meeting, people talk
About Jerusalem, and talking sing of peace,
        Their only greeting.

123 Mercy

I look to the sky, and wait
For a hand to reach down
Through a window, a cloud,
And I wait. Like drought land
Rutted, cracked with contempt
For the easy, with scorn for the proud
Tanning nude, we want rain.
Tip your hand.
We will wait.

157

∞

Return.
Promise.

124   Social

Without help we'd be gone:
In a flash when the angry ones turn up their flames:
Not a gurgle as floodwaters swallow our souls.
   Bless the Lord, for our souls
Are those songbirds set free from the snares,
From nets fowlers baited. Without help
   We join flocks, or alight.

125   *Please*

As mountains ring Jerusalem
So God surrounds the people,
Chosen by heart, not by lot.
They are cedars on mountains.

Wind twists the evil ones, fearful.
High hills protect Israel.

159

∽

Return.
Promise.

126 Reasoning

When we returned from far away
Our home looked as it looks in dreams:
The sun shines, gates swing
Open of themselves, and someone
Sings a song we had forgotten
As we now remember laughter.
Then strangers said, Great things
Were done for them.

160

                              The Lord
Did great things for us then. A good.
But you must do great things again,

Book
Five

Because we live with heaviness
And twist and scatter like a river
Delta bogged in marsh and reeds.
We started sadly so we'd end up
Smiling, for anyone begins, sows
Seed with tears to reap his own,
The happy harvest, no?

127 Pointed

Live for yourself, live for nothing:
A city of watchers and waiters,
Of early birds, burners of night lights, of eaters
Of what gets dished up by the loaf and the spoonful
Are loveless, fitful sleepers, wanting children.
Children ransom the hostage, the happy man,
One who grows up with them, old with them:
Early they take to the walks; watch them later
Stand in their doorways talking to children of strangers.   *161*

Return.
Promise.

128 Thrive

Daughter and wife, blessings
I never thought of alone
In the city relying on money:

Winter sun streams on the bayberries,
Fallow beds, orchard buds, hedge,
Gates to the heart's Jerusalem.

∞

129 Harvest

"They treated me like dirt while I was growing up,"
Israel says. "They walked all over me.
They plowed my back into a fallow, furrowed field."
Snap their yoke, Lord. Beat the haters into thatch
Too dry for harvesting, unfit for brooms,
And make those sweeping past not know the way
To speak a blessing in your name.

163

∞

Return.
Promise.

130   Interior

Deep down I call out
To you, O God:
Hear me. Don't keep
My slips always before
You, before me, or who
Could survive here?

I wait for the answer
That's more
Than an echo,
God, harder
Than daylight,
And kinder, and longer.

131 Hushed

I don't look too high, aiming
To muddle big questions: still
A small child, my soul has been weaned
From the breast and the bottle,
And taught to behave, understand.
So I hope.

165

∞

Return.
Promise.

132   Gradual

David swore he would not rest until the Ark was carried
Out from Obed-edom's house, where David left it,
Through the main gate to Jerusalem.

Levites took the Ark upon their shoulders, following
The dancing King of Israel, who beat his tambourine
And sang: Come up, come up.
                              Then God swore back:

    Your sons and their sons' sons will sit
        On Zion's throne:
Jerusalem will be my home, and when
        Your children practice
My law, learn those lessons taught
        Discerning hearts,
The poor shall have their bread,
        The wise know pleasure:
They will sing and dance and blow the horn
        At new year. Lamps burn
Oil. Your enemies will blush with rage
        Because you flourish.

133 *Singular*

Different peoples, families at peace with one another are like
Oil poured atop the head that curls behind the ears and down
    the front of Aaron's beard to his robed ankles, are like
Dew on Hermon, beads rolled down the sides of Zion's
    mountains where, commanded, we chose good, and life.

167

∞

Return.
Promise.

134 Late

A scholar at his desk at midnight
Looked up from his book, beyond the lamplight,
Into a socked-in yard where gray wisps swirled
Between clotheslines, and said: Blessed be the creator
    of this world.

135 Residence

I stood on the front porch,
Admired the juniper, lily bed, privet hedge screening the street.
    This house feels separate, chosen.
Blue sky framed by trees seems much deeper, the sea breeze
    More tempered than on open beach,
      Where black clouds spit lightning, strong gusts
Clap waves dragging sand out, walk dunes into nothing.

The firstborn of Egypt were sucked into darkness.   169
The living remainder watched Israel's passage   ∞
Across empty places that did not show footprints,
Across famous kingdoms once mighty in Canaan: *Return.*
Of Sihon the Amorite, of Og, King of Bashan: *Promise.*
Their land was a promise, a gift to our children.

If even a man's word lasts longer than buildings,
Then rumors of God have more substance than idols:
    Stone lips speak no doctrine,
    Gold eyes show no vision,
    Brass ears ring no phrases,
    Silver tongues taste no lilting
    In praise of their maker,
Or makers, just like them, who trust them.

God bless Jacob's children, and listen to Aaron's:
Those living in cities, and parents who fear for them,
    Speak for them, living in Zion.

Thank the Lord, there is good in life
　　　Always returning
Thank the Lord there is just one god
　　　Always returning
Thank the Lord there are many ways
　　　Always returning
One who makes wondering
　　　Always returning
One who knows sky as mind
　　　Always returning
Set gem land in ocean rings
　　　Always returning
Who mounted the living lights
　　　Always returning
The sun to show daytime
　　　Always returning
Moon and stars steering nights
　　　Always returning
Who smote Egypt's firstborn
　　　Always returning
Led Israel's children out
　　　Always returning
Played strong hand at arms' length
　　　Always returning
Who parted the Red Sea reeds
　　　Always returning
A causeway for Israel
　　　Always returning

170

∞

Book
Five

But swallowed up following Pharaoh and chariots
        Always returning
Whose pillar led people through desert waste
        Always returning
Who toppled old kingdoms
        Always returning
Who killed famous rulers,
        Always returning
Crushed Sihon of Heshbon,
        Always returning
Erased Og of Bashan,
        Always returning
Gave their lands to our fathers,
        Always returning
His children of Israel
        Always returning
Who remembered us, sunken hulks
        Always returning
And floated us, salvaged and
        Always returning
Who finds food for all living things
        Always returning
Thank the Lord there is one God, good
        Always returning

∞

Return.

Promise.

137   *Even*

In Babel, where the tower fell, strangers
Do not speak our language. We were taken
There in chains and, captive by the rivers,
Told to sing them songs of Zion. Crushed,
Could we sing Hebrew praises in translation?

Even happy, when our children asked us
Why this bread was eaten, and rehearsed
The plagues God rained on Egypt's head, we hope
To see Jerusalem. Jerusalem,
My tongue would stick between my teeth,
My right hand palsy, before I forget you.

Lord, remember when your city fell,
The Chaldees chanting
"Sack her, strip her, raze her to the ground" —
Babylon, you jackal's daughter, happy
Is the one to pay you back in kind:
Who will smash your babies' heads against the rocks.

When I heard what my heart said
First I looked outside: Two horses
Trotted out stone gargoyle gates.
They rode away.
              If nothing's written
In the heart, then try the book
That's never blank. Enter, sound
Of hoofbeats. (Wood blocks clop.)

173

∞

Return.

Promise.

139 Recognition

Look in:
My soul is glass
To you, no vein
Or bone unseen,
But you know
All I pass through,
All I do, ahead
Or inside me,
Before I do.
I can't tell
What you don't
Prompt my tongue
To say, no matter what
The thought: no cloak
So thick, no parcel
Of the sky (if I
Made wings this morning),
No ditch, no deep
(Were I to dive
Or dig) so dark
That your hand could not
Find me, touch me,
Seize me, raise me
Gasping, flashing
Scales to the light.
My soul's a tiny
You, my bones your
Bread baked in ovens
Buried under foot,

My days unreeled
Film you took in
At a glance before
I lived them. If my songs
Outnumbered sea grass
Grown on sand dunes
Inching inland from the margin,
They would count less
Than a comma, than a swash
Stroked in your book. Both
Of and with you, have I ever
Cottoned to bad ones
Lugging bags of goods,
Who worship their bodies,
Who lie and act tasteful?
I think not. I hate them
And refuse their cash,
Their compliments, their statuettes
And solemn uniforms.
Peer through the glass,
Lord, know me, show
Me a right way to walk
My watch on your part
In the daylight, into night.

∞

Return.
Promise.

140   *Spray*

Violence, slander, snakes
Spit poison, gossip, forked
Tongues plot war.

Don't let them trip me up
On my own laces or
In pits they've dug.

I said, Hear me, God.
Don't make my words sound
Empty. Keep me

Living, rain hot lava
On their flat heads, scorch
Shut drivel lips.

Wipe bully-smeared dung from
Your face. Just flick it off.
Leave us. Be praised.

141 Taught

Smoke whispers up the landlocked sky.
    Come early, Lord, come sooner:
Nodding heads snap to attention at the rapped
    Desk, where a beam of sunlight
Holds its chalkline to the globe. Once bones
    Were bound in cords, stacked,
Strewn by stokers, scattered like white dandelion
    Seeds, made chalk or lime.
A fowler's twig. Dear God, next time take
    Grackles only in their net.

177

∞

Return.
Promise.

142   *Aloud*

I said the thing out loud
    And to the Lord.
I bowed down, I complained
    About my troubles:

When I was lost, and did not know
    Where to turn
Away from traps the plotters set
    Along my way,
Just breathing was an act of will.
    Look right or left:
All, all alone in danger,
    Grown a stranger
To ones who knew me once.
    An orphaned soul,
I raised my voice to you:

    O Lord, my help
And place among the living,
    Hear me.
I am lower than the least
    Of those who wait
Upon my happy enemies.
    Let my soul
Out of this cage, so I can freely
    Sing your name
In company with friends, in truth.
    Your hand is open.

143 Distinction

I can't cry innocent in any court:
Dogged by enemies, I ran, was caught.
Pitched in a hole, my soul turned waste,
Heart hollow rock not even wind might whistle through.
Did darkness, when the universe was torn from you
　　Into its being, long for nothing?

Hurry. Faces of the long departed, dim and empty,
Peer up from the pit. I said, "The sun will rise tomorrow.   179
I will see it." Will I? Keep me and my spirits spinning   ∞
Level at the rim until the hateful clatter echoless
Down their appointed slot. Then keep me longer: *Return.*
　　No good likeness when I am not.   *Promise.*

My fingers twang the bowstring.
Arrows flying from the tower
Land whole armies at my feet.
What is one human,
That God should know or care about him or his children?
Steam clouds, shadows in the air.
Lightning makes the mountains smoke;
Broken sunlight, rainbows.

Nock your shafts, Lord, fix
Those strangers speaking languages
With no word for truth,
Who hold one hand out, fingers crossed behind their back.
Teach me to pluck the heartstring, sing
Like David did before
Those strangers speaking languages
With no word for truth.
Set our sons in glazed
Enamelled tile patterns, inlaid
Daughters, walls and pillars.
Keep our pantries stocked with meat, fruit, grain, and drink.
Let no guest uninvited, come,
Nor welcomed, go.
When miseries shout in the street,
Take them in hand.

Allow us,
Blessed
Creator,

Dancing
Exits,
Free from

Gravity
(Heaven
Is just

Knowing
Life less
Matter);

Operatic
Passions'
Quavers;

Reason's
Slender
Tapers;

Unstaged vigils'
Waxy
Zeal.

181

Return.
Promise.

146   First

Just being, being born, just crossing
From the wings, however long, is praise.
On stage I thought, spoke, sung, alone, before
A hall packed by an audience of one.
Practice made us help and hope for heaven.
Time and all that's in them keep the weak,
Bent, put-upon alive to promises like justice.
Part the curtain. Nations slip out between phrases
On the coral lips of oceans breaking over reefs,
Earth square and settled under winter rain.

182

∞

Book

Five

147   *Who Else?*

But the Lord rebuilds Jerusalem,
Collects the scattered, cast-off, brokenhearted
Seed of Israel and knows how many
Stars there are, and calls them all
By name, and hears the answer.
We can't describe how music works
Or know the time of clouds, rain, mountain grass.
Cattle graze there, crows pick
Through what horses leave behind.
A rider strong enough to pass through air
Needs more than skill to master fear.
When earth becomes Jerusalem, praise
Doors that keep the north wind out,
Your children warm inside, with bread, fruit
Of the plain unrolling thunder, tables
Where wool snow blankets ashes, frost
Nips hail-sown buds of cold. A glance.
They melt, soft breezes streaming water.
Only we have heard it, and retell it.

183

∽

Return.
Promise.

148 Zeal

We people are more
Recent than creation's rumor.
Aimless desert nomad shepherds' children,
Island in a sea of nations, reading dreamers
Steered by whispers, we stand on years
Eternity a moment, then disappear.

Time's two hands, give and take,
Hold fire and ice and clay and darkness,
Everything you can imagine, and make

Lions of our own device. But not alone,
O Lord. We play short rags on dragon deeps,
Raised by the stories that were always old, gone
Days past telling sung to you as praise, for keeps.

New song? Nearly. Better
Hums through a kazoo than fancy fretwork
    Strums to dazzle children.
Echoes in the shower, muffled bedroom
    Cries: a two-edged sword:
It cuts the mute and those who should know better.
    Writers without spirit
Cannot even praise the letter truly.

185

∞

Return.
Promise.

150   Last

Vaulted ceilings echo, raise
The trumpet, organ, ram's horn,
Harp and lute for finger dancers,
Tambourine, bowed viols, buzzing
Double reeds, flutes, clapping cymbals,
Drumbeats, singing, humming, breathing
    Close to what they praise.

∾